praise for
the story of with

"Allen Arnold has created a transformative experience. **Unique and powerful, The Story of With will take readers deep into the discovery of their own identity.** Bravo! This fascinating blend of storytelling and teaching will shift the thinking of all who take the journey."

—TED DEKKER
New York Times Bestselling Author

"I am so thankful for this book. Through allegory and invitation, Allen Arnold ushers us into **a journey of imagination, insight, wonder, and wisdom.** Will we live in partnership with God as His child or as an orphan, searching for a life that is beyond the bounds of our own ability to attain? Read *The Story of With!* As I did, you will recognize yourself in these pages and be called to the more you long for."

—STASI ELDREDGE
New York Times Bestselling Co-Author of *Captivating*

"**Allen has written a roadmap for dreaming with God. The Story of With is a beautiful revelatory parable, filled with wonder, mystery and adventure.** I was often stirred to remember that with God, all impossibilities are possible. If you have lost your way or are navigating between hope and heart-sickness, *The Story of With* is for you. It is a transformational book that will inspire you to live *fulfilled* in hope."

—JASON CLARK
Author of *Prone To Love* & *Untamed*
Lead Communicator at AFamilyStory.org

"We all have at least one thing, (or a hundred) that we'd like to improve, change or simply rid ourselves of. **This allegory gives us practical tools, while entertaining us, and reminding us that our best way to freedom is to actually free ourselves from ourselves and let God in.** It's a story that truly takes us somewhere new and brings us back changed and prepared for the dreams and goals we've put aside for too long. Allen Arnold has tapped into some core issues of all of us that want more, but expect it differently than we get it."

—JAMES ARNOLD TAYLOR
Actor/Entertainer/Speaker (Voice of Obi-Wan Kenobi,
Fred Flintstone, Ratchet, Johnny Test)

"In a world where so many are merely surviving, Allen Arnold hands us an inspired invitation. **Through clever use of allegory, *The Story of With* not only challenges the status quo, it awakens us to a new way, a better way, a vital way of living and creating.** It is water for the wrung dry, fresh air for the overwhelmed, and courage for all. I am forever changed by this message."

—KATIE GANSHERT
Award-winning Author of *The Art of Losing Yourself*

"For the seeking. The secretly discontent. The wandering, restless hearts. *The Story of With* is for you. As a former jet-setting corporate consultant for a Fortune-100 Company, this book came at the perfect time in my career-change journey. Allen's words proved inspiring, and carried **a message of presence with God over productivity that will mend the hearts of creatives and calling-seekers everywhere. A must-read book for anyone desiring a closer walk WITH God."**

—KRISTY CAMBRON
Award-winning Author of *The Ringmaster's Wife*
and *A Hidden Masterpiece* series

the story of
WITH

A Better Way to Live, Love, & Create

An Allegory

ALLEN ARNOLD

Unless otherwise noted, Scripture quotations are taken from
The Message by Eugene H. Peterson. © 1993, 1994, 1995, 1996, 2000.
Used by permission of NavPress Publishing Group. All rights reserved.

Printed in the United States of America

ISBN: 978-0-692-76958-4

Third Edition

10 9 8 7 6 5 4 3

To Kellye—
My wife and love.
You show me the beauty of presence over
productivity and the importance of
being more rather than simply doing more.
To bigger dreams and more life…together.

contents

foreword

Dear Reader,

The fact you've picked this book up says maybe—just maybe—you're hoping for something more. More perspective. More creativity. More freedom. More to this life and the future than what our culture and climate so easily promise but too often fail to provide.

So let me assure you right now…you are in the right place.

In fact, if I could offer anything to prepare you it would simply be to stop, breathe, and *be you* for a moment. Be *in* this moment—separate from the ocean of busy and voices that need everything from you.

You are not alone.

Whether you're a free spirit, office exec, a writer, musician, college student, or tired parent—your soul, like mine, knows life is meant to go beyond rat-races and rare applause. This book speaks to that belief. And if you're not careful, you may find tears warming your eyes as you read because finally someone is naming your weariness, your striving, your questions of why you just can't quite make it, or the emptiness that hit because maybe you *did*. It is into those places *The Story of With* reaches—fusing allegory with application—to offer fresh perspective, restored hope, and a rebirth of creativity.

And good grief isn't that what you want? The wonder of a life fully experienced, instead of just strived after or survived.

I've read this book upward of seven times in one form or another, from notes to completion (I clearly needed it, ha). And each version has come right as my soul felt dry, or crabby, or hungry for something I couldn't quite place. Whether in the midst of writing my own novels with no creativity left, or when the rejections and producing felt overwhelming, or the days I hoped

I was just succeeding at being a decent human / worker / mom / wife / girl. In that way, not only has this story of Allen Arnold's helped shape my own writing, but it's helped shape my soul and understanding of who I am as a child of the King. Which I'm convinced these days is something we need to hear now more than ever.

So come join me, friend. Pull up a chair around the fire, and feast on a story of MORE. Take notes. Take heart. And let this book be a warm blanket for your soul as you are welcomed home to the place you always knew existed.

—Mary Weber
Christy & Carol Award-Winning,
Scholastic Pick Author of the *Storm Siren* Trilogy

*"I'll be a Father to you;
you'll be sons and daughters to me."*

The Message (2 Corinthians 6:18)

*"Wherever you have dreamed of going, I have
camped there, and left firewood for when you arrive."*

Hafiz

*"We walk every day on the razor edge between
these two incredible possibilities. Apparently, then,
our lifelong nostalgia, our longing to be reunited with
something in the universe from which we now feel cut
off, to be on the inside of some door which we have
always seen from the outside, is no mere neurotic
fancy, but the truest index of our real situation.
And to be at last summoned inside would be both
glory and honor beyond all our merits and also
the healing of that old ache."*

C.S. Lewis, *The Weight of Glory*[1]

1. *The Weight of Glory*, by C.S. Lewis, New York: The Macmillan Company, 1949

PART ONE

hunger
for
more

How The Fortune Cookie Crumbled

Most of us are stuck in a story of *without*. We go about our tasks and get through the day without much hope, without our dreams realized, without deep friendships, and without experiencing the presence of God.

> Most of us are stuck in a story of *without*.

For decades, I couldn't put words to how these missing pieces affected my life. But the result was a slow erosion of passion and a pull to what I felt I was able to control. If it were all up to me, then I would figure out the formula for the best possible life.

I was successful by the world's standards. Yet even in the moments when everything appeared good, an indescribable ache tugged at my soul. It was an emptiness that success couldn't satisfy coupled with a vague hope that there had to be more.

From the outside, I was on the fast track to the top. I began my career at some of the nation's most acclaimed advertising agencies. I later founded the fiction division at a top-ten publishing house. My role was to acquire talented storytellers and help bring their ideas to life. And it worked big time. I was recognized in a prestigious "40 under 40" publishing industry list as one of the top forty visionaries under age 40.

From a soul perspective, however, I was in a free fall to rock bottom.

I was an extremely driven man in search of a larger story. And then one day I thought I found the answer after a meal of Kung Pao chicken. Usually fortune cookies offer forgettable clichés, but not this time. The message inside this one put words to a worldview I resonated with: *"The one who says it can't be done should get out of the way of the one already doing it."*

It's not wise to take your life mantra from a fortune cookie, but I taped this one to my desk. More than that, I embraced it as truth. My worth would be in what I did. And I would be the one to make the impossible happen.

During my twenties and thirties, I felt I could open any door through sheer force of will. What seemed extreme to others was energizing to me. And the problem was, it was working.

Staring Down a Plane

What started as a normal workday quickly turned into a case of man versus plane. This event took place long before 9/11—at a time when airport security was far less than it is today. Otherwise, it may have been the last story of my life.

I was on a business call as I awaited my flight when I looked up to see the boarding area completely empty. I ran to the gate. "I have to get on that plane. I have an important meeting and my video crew is already on board."

"Your seat has been given to a standby passenger," the attendant said. "The plane has already left."

I looked through the large plate glass windows behind her at the runway. "Turn around and look," I pleaded. "The plane is right there. I've got to get on it."

"You're too late. You missed it," she said and walked away.

Where others would have conceded defeat, I was undeterred. I took a deep breath, pushed open the emergency exit door to the tarmac, and walked toward the runway as the alarm blared. I approached the small commuter plane, unsure what would happen next. I didn't have to wonder long. The pilot barged out of the plane, straight for me.

His bewilderment was no match for my singular determination to board the plane. Minutes later, the standby passenger was escorted off. The video crew couldn't believe what they had just witnessed. "Dude, you stared down a plane and it blinked first." I found the open seat and started reading a book, victorious and oblivious to the havoc I'd caused for everyone on the flight. Against the odds, I had made it happen. Now let's get this flight going.

I cringe at that story now. I was the bull in the china shop who relentlessly forced his way forward regardless of the cost. And there was always a cost—to my wife, my coworkers, and though unseen for years, my heart.

Several promotions later, I led a marketing team that initiated hundreds of national book campaigns. We were experiencing a season of immense success. One Friday, my boss invited me to what I thought was a casual lunch. Before taking the first bite of my sandwich, he began. "Allen, do you realize everyone on your team thinks you're a jerk?" His actual language was more colorful—and he was just getting started. "Not one of them enjoys being in your presence. They can't stand being around you. They only stay because you're good at what you do."

It was the last thing I expected, a sucker punch to the gut. Didn't he understand how challenging it was to keep these people in line? Wasn't he happy with the results? Sure, I was relentless with my expectations, but no more than I was on myself. I was the one who made things happen. And I was delivering success. Wasn't that what mattered?

> I was delivering success. Wasn't that what mattered?

I stared at my boss, wanting to defend myself. Yet no words came. So I sat back and took it in. And in that moment, something in me shifted. I saw myself as others did, and I no longer wanted to be that man.

Chasing fast after the wrong definitions of success does accomplish one thing. It causes you to reach the end of yourself and the illusion of control sooner rather than later. I felt deep shame at who I was . . . but also a glimmer of hope in who I could become.

I believed God could make all things new . . . I just never realized it was me who needed to be made new. Though slowly at first, I began to see that God would father me if I simply allowed myself to be a son. I no longer had to have all the answers. My validation wasn't tied to the approval of others. My goal wasn't to get my to-do list completed, but simply to do whatever I did with God.

Over time, a fellowship of others came alongside me and helped me chart a better path. I would begin anew—no longer focused on building my own kingdom. Instead, as a restored King I would use whatever power I was given to care for those under my authority.

More than a decade later, I joined a ministry in Colorado. My supervisor welcomed me with these words: "Allen, we know you can get things done. But we want you for your presence—not your productivity." It was as if time stood still. I had come full circle from the conversation in the deli with my other boss. I had become a new man. And it all began with a disruptive invitation to *be* more, rather than *do* more.

Your Missing Super Powers

Maybe you've never been that driven. Perhaps you struggle with passivity. But can we agree something important has been lost? Even if you can't put your finger on it, there's a yearning inside, a sense that there has to be more.

I was recently waiting for a friend at a large gathering. Beside me was the Lost and Found bin. A woman walked up, peered in, and sorted through the various items. As she left empty-handed, she quipped, "Just seeing if my super powers were in there."

Exactly!

Something essential has gone missing. You've just been searching for it in the wrong place.

This is good news. It means you're not crazy for feeling that way. And it gets better. Because what's lost can be found—once you know where to look for it.

> Something essential has gone missing. You've just been searching for it in the wrong place.

What if this untapped strength we've lost track of is hidden in plain sight? What if the answer lies within our distinct desires, talents, and creativity? Could the God of all Creation have placed inside us, before we were even born, a homing device that ultimately would lead us back to Him? In other words, could the one thing we're most passionate about and skilled at doing also reveal the way to more life, love, and creativity?

That's not what the world teaches us. From childhood, it seems the message is that creativity is rare and reserved for the elite few. While it would be nice if everyone possessed a unique ability or talent, we're told that most folks didn't receive that secret sauce at birth.

But what if we did? What if *you* did?

For the moment, simply reorient yourself to this truth. You. Are. Creative.

Perhaps this doesn't feel true. You've not yet experienced this reality. Or you may have been met with rejection when you share your unique talents with others.

But you are creative.

How could it be otherwise? Your bloodline traces back beyond your parents. The DNA of the Creator pulses through you. And the One who created sunsets, oceans, stars, and laughter cannot create something that doesn't have His eternal spark within it. He does not make generically creative beings. He wove into each of us a specific set of interests, passions, and curiosity—which holds clues to our greater destiny and our truer selves.

The answer isn't simply in discovering your creative gift. Many know and pursue their talents daily. If successful, it is how they are defined . . . or come to define themselves. And yet the hunger persists. There has to be more than simply understanding what you can do well.

Perhaps you have been told or believe that you aren't creative, which also has enormous consequences. It closes a door to a future shaped by what you were born to bring into existence through your unique presence and talents.

Some of our dreams have been met with disinterest. Others with applause. Outwardly, these responses appear to be on opposite ends of the spectrum, yet both have the same foundation. They are tethered to human validation. Over time, we begin to chase the approval of others rather than our original dreams.

> Over time, we begin to chase the approval of others rather than our original dreams.

To counter this pull, you have to go back to why you were given your gifts in the first place. It wasn't to win the approval of others. Your specific interests and talents are actually more powerful than that. They offer a gateway to discover your truer identity. And an entirely new way to pursue your dreams.

> The first step in seeing with new eyes is to let go of the belief that our current reality is the only reality.

If God weaves specific talents into each of us, the question is *why?* What is His motive? I believe He gives each of us a particular calling so He can then spend time with us on that unique playground. This is a way for you and God to get to know each other better as you create together.

Yet clearly something is missing. Because what I just described isn't the way most people pursue their gifting or dreams.

What Fish Can't See

The problem comes when we limit what's possible to what's probable. The first step in seeing with new eyes is to let go of the belief that our current reality is the only reality.

How would you explain the ocean to a goldfish still in his bowl? He was born in a small container with invisible glass walls that define—and limit—his potential. He's a captive who thinks he is free. Swimming circles in his small world has led to small dreams. He thinks the best he can hope for is a bigger bowl when what he needs are bigger dreams. Because an ocean awaits.

What would you see if you could stand outside your current circumstances? Stated another way, who would you be if the world didn't tell you who you are?

> ## Who would you be if the world didn't tell you who you are?

Though few live from this space, it is possible to walk through each day with a sense of knowing who you are and how that identity connects you to the most important desires, people, and events of your life. You can experience a sense of expectancy in the midst of interruptions, knowing the unplanned can lead to something better than anything you could have planned. Imagine stepping into your relationships and creativity with a power that isn't limited to your solutions or strength?

This is the opposite of what we've been taught since childhood. As children, we naturally gravitated to what brought us joy. But as we grew, we discovered that the way to get ahead was to do what the world (or those we loved) applauded. So we began to pursue our relationships and work according to this matrix. Yet, we eventually realized that something about this approach was wrong. Because the more we based our worth on what we did, the less we became. We shifted from the overachiever to the overwhelmed. Though this cycle may define your world, it doesn't have to remain your world. There is a better way.

What Adventurers Know

Explorers and adventurers understand a great truth. In order to experience the fantastic, they have to first put themselves in fantastic places. It is the same for us.

Conversely, if we rely solely on common sense, we experience a common life.

The last thing we want is more of the status quo. What's needed is an infusion of the fantastical. A shift into something so beyond our dreams that it could only be seen as miraculous.

I'm not suggesting you jump off a cliff and ask God to miraculously provide wings as you fall to the ground. That's not faith. It's foolishness. What I am encouraging you to do is to let go of your preconceived notions of what is possible and ask God about His dreams for you. They will likely be far bigger than anything you've yet imagined. But remember, God will never say anything that goes against what He has already said in Scripture. And especially for large decisions, you want a close circle of strong believers to listen for you as well.

Once you know God is inviting you into more, you have a choice. You can either run with Him or run from Him. In those circumstances, the only way to experience a miracle is to put yourself in a position to need one. That is part of stepping into dreams so big that only God can make them come true.

But how do we do this?

> The only way to experience a miracle is to put yourself in a position to need one.

The Reality of Realms

What if all that has held you back isn't your fault? What if you're simply living in the wrong realm? We all spend our lives in one of two places. We can't alternate from one to the other, like trying on a new pair of clothes. The two are actually in fierce opposition to each other.

Your realm is the place where you exist. It colors how you interpret everything about your life. It's your outlook or perspective. It affects how you see yourself and how others feel when they are around you. It influences what you pursue and what pursues you. It has a huge impact on your identity and your imagination. Each realm even has its own language of bondage or freedom.

This explains why people react so differently in similar circumstances. Yes, it's partially due to

Your realm is the place where you exist. It colors how you interpret everything about your life.

who they are. But who they are is shaped by the realm they live in. The bad news is we all begin in the wrong realm. The good news is we don't have to stay there. We get to choose where we exist.

The Shift to "With"

In the first realm, we live and pursue life as if it were all up to us. Whether we fail or succeed, we do it in our own strength. That means we only have ourselves to blame or to credit. It is a place of doing more—because we're evaluated on what we do. I call this the Orphan Realm and I was a long-term resident there.

Those who live in this place go through life overwhelmed, disheartened, and isolated. In other words: alone. Our bosses, our leaders, and even our spouses convey (often unintentionally) that the way to *be* more is to *do* more. Yet the more we give, the more is demanded of us. We end up losing ourselves in the expectations of others. We realize no matter how much we give, it is never enough. The path we thought would be satisfying eventually sucks the marrow from our weary bones.

You can believe in God and still miss life with Him. You can know about God and still live as an Orphan.

The goal isn't just to escape what isn't working, it's to be free from that way of living. The foundational shift requires moving from a life of independence and self-reliance to a life wholly dependent on God. I understand how this may sound passive if you're used to making things happen. Yet it is actually an extremely courageous decision that invites you into an unscripted life without limits. God sees farther and better than you. Why not run with Him instead of alone in the dark?

> You can believe in God and still miss life with Him. You can know about God and still live as an Orphan.

Living with a dependence on God and not on yourself is only available in the second realm—a place where we pursue our life, love, and creativity *with* God. I've named this the Freedom Realm. We will discover more about this realm as we continue on our journey.

The Invitation

God has turned my world upside down in the most counterintuitive ways. He's shown me the futility of trying to make life work on my own. As Scottish poet and novelist George MacDonald (1824–1905) notes: "In whatever a man does without God, he must fail miserably—or succeed more miserably."[2]

Life *without* God leads to misery. The key is relationship. Yet so many who believe in God miss the experience of life *with* Him.

> Life *without* God leads to misery. The key is relationship. Yet so many who believe in God miss the experience of life *with* Him.

As I allowed God to father me, He gave me a new life mission: pursue the hearts

---

2. George MacDonald, *Unspoken Sermons, Series I, II, III* (Johannesen Classic Edition, 1997).

of those living like orphans and awaken them to their core identity as His sons and daughters.

That is why I've written this book. I could have filled it with facts and formulas. But doing so would bore both of us. So instead, I'd like to tell you a story.

Just as explorers travel to fantastical places in search of the unknown, stories can transport us to places where we can then see our own stories more clearly. They invite us into other worlds and, in the process, offer a new way of seeing our own world.

Stories speak to our hearts in ways that facts alone fall short. Like when tears come unexpectedly while watching a movie. Or when a song you haven't heard in a decade provokes a forgotten longing.

We underestimate stories when we see them as just an escape from reality or a vehicle to teach a lesson. We don't need to escape our lives—nor do we need more lessons. We need our hearts awakened. And nothing reaches the heart faster than story.

So rather than offer more theories or principles, I give you this story. Like a meal worth savoring, we'll pause after each chapter for you to catch your breath and consider what's going on at a heart level.

For too long, we've lived without hopes and dreams. There is a better way.

It is the story of *with*.

PART TWO
– an allegory –

the
blue
door

dreams

Mia wished her father could be with her in this moment, but she had to get through this on her own. She wasn't even sure why she still thought of him. He'd left a long time ago.

The lanky twenty-nine year old ran her hand through her auburn hair. She had to stay focused. Too much was riding on this interview to get lost in childhood regrets.

She'd spent the last three hours at Strava Food Group's headquarters sitting at a boardroom table answering rapid-fire questions in the hopes of making their manager-training program. Being a waitress paid the bills, but this was her best hope to advance in her culinary career. Now it appeared her fate rested with this four-person committee. Like everything in life, she had to earn her place or be cut.

A man with tiny spectacles looked over his file folder. "We need a few minutes to arrive at our decision." As if on cue, the boardroom door opened and a man in chocolate brown slacks, cobalt blue dress shirt, and red silk tie stood at attention. "Mr. Dunbar will give you a tour of our world-class facilities while we talk."

The man nodded at Mia. "You can call me Brandon. Come this way." Though they'd told her to dress comfortably for this meeting, Mia felt a little too casual in jeans and a peasant top.

While the committee compared notes, she was shown the inner workings of their empire. Mia strove to keep pace in her wedge sandals as her guide sped through the test kitchen. "This is where we experiment with potential recipes and restaurant concepts before they get the green light. We demand the most efficient solutions."

She slowed to watch one of the workers drizzle glaze over a large metal pan of mini-waffles. Another dusted it with a sifter of powdered sugar. It reminded her of the times as a girl when she and her dad would cook breakfast on Saturday mornings. She'd get more sugar on her clothes than the waffles. The white coat before her read directions from a monitor, her brow furrowed and her lips pressed in a tight line, resembling a lab technician more than a chef.

Her guide. Where did he go? There. He was heading into the next area. She was about to apologize when she realized he hadn't even noticed her absence. He continued his monologue without a backward glance.

He paused and straightened his tie before the large sign above the main preparation area. "We take our responsibility here seriously. This reminds our workers that there is nothing more important than knowing what to do and doing it well."

Mia raised her eyes to the sign.

---

4 Questions

What are you doing?

What should you be doing & why aren't you doing that?

How can you do more?

When are you going to start?

He studied her expression as she read the sign. "Is there a problem?"

"No. Well, I mean, the math is wrong."

"Excuse me?"

"The sign says four questions. But there are five."

His lips formed a tight smile. "So there are." He pulled out a notepad and jotted a few words before resuming his fast pace.

As they finished the tour, he opened the boardroom door. "Have a seat. The committee will be back soon with their decision."

Mia stood in the lavish room with a large mahogany table at the center. She sunk into one of the brown leather chairs. She had pre-pared for this meeting for weeks, reading the two hundred-page binder on the company's history and growth philosophy. It was a lucra-tive business model. After all, people had to eat. Every day. And the Strava Food Group controlled every step of the dining experience, trademarking their recipes, monitoring the cost of each ingredient, and maximizing the number of people they served.

She loved to cook. And they loved to make money by feeding people. Training to be a manager of one of their restaurants would at least allow her to be around food . . . even if she wasn't the one creating the dishes.

Her cell phone vibrated on the smooth conference table. It was Sara, a waitress she worked with.

"Hey, I've got to talk fast. What's up?"

The voice on the other end of the phone quivered. "I lost my job, Mia. So did half the waitstaff."

Mia took a deep breath. Sara was a single mom with two girls. "I can't believe they fired you."

"Doug said it isn't personal. There's just not enough business. Um, Mia, I called because he needs to talk to you too."

Her stomach tightened. She was so focused on Sara's plight that she hadn't considered what the news might mean for her.

A new voice came on the line. "It's been a long day, Mia, so I'll keep this short. You got lucky. You still have your job, for now."

Tears welled in her eyes. To say she lived paycheck to paycheck was an understatement. More like minute to minute. Hopefully all that would change when the committee came back and invited her into their management program.

"Doug, I—"

"Don't go mushy on me. I flipped a coin to decide who stayed and who got let go. Like I said, you got lucky."

"But what about Sara?"

"You tryin' to tell me how to do my job? Let it go, Mia. What's done is done."

"But I just thought—"

He huffed. "You know what, I'll give her your job. Happy now?"

"Wait, that's not what I—"

"We're done. I've got a restaurant to run." The line went dead.

She stared at the beige boardroom wall. After waiting tables for two years, she'd lost her job in a one-minute phone call? The committee's decision just took on infinitely more weight. It was all that stood between her and being evicted from her apartment when the rent came due next week. She was already one month behind.

She heard the door open and the man with the spectacles entered and sat across from her, his face expressionless.

"Where is everyone else?"

He cleared his throat. "They are conducting another interview at the moment. As you

know, Strava Food Group is a rapidly growing organization. The future is very bright for
everyone here."

Mia fidgeted with her silver and turquoise
necklace. She needed this to work.

"What I'm saying is, we are the best . . . and
we hire the best."

"I understand." Mia leaned in. "I've taken
classes at the Culinary Institute and have worked
at a large restaurant, I know I'm qualified. Maybe
overqualified. Is that what you're thinking?"

"Not exactly." He took off his glasses
and twirled them in his left hand. "We have
decided to pass on you."

Mia felt light-headed, yet fought to stay
focused. "Please. I know I can do this. I've
loved to cook since I was a girl. I understand
how meals can bring people together. I—"

He closed the folder and glanced at his
watch. "There's nothing more to discuss. At
every stage of our business, we demand the
best. It's not that you were a poor choice, Mia.
There are just much better options before us."

"So that's it?"

"Since you asked, I'll offer this last piece of
advice. Stop chasing some childhood dream.

The world doesn't work that way. This isn't about what you loved to do as a girl. It's about getting things done."

Just hold it together until you get to the car.

He held his hand out. "Nothing personal, Meg."

"My name is Mia." She walked out of the boardroom, leaving his hand unshaken.

Inside her old Chevy Nova, Mia lowered her head to the steering wheel and allowed the tears to flow. She'd been a fool. Somehow she believed that she could actually find work doing what she loved. But she was fired as a waitress and couldn't make the cut for a restaurant training program. Who cares if she enjoys cooking?

She pressed her palms into her eyes and rubbed the emotion away. *Toughen up, girl. Another dream gone. Get used to it.*

She started the car, cranked up the stereo, and punched the accelerator. The four-hour drive would give her time to figure something out. She thought of her friend and sighed. *At least Sara still has her job.*

As she approached the interstate, it was bumper-to-bumper traffic. The flashing sign at the entrance ramp read: Expect Delays. Accident Ahead. Mia glanced at the map app on her phone. It offered an alternate route that took backroads for seventeen miles. Fine. She'd take the detour and reconnect with the interstate once she was past whatever was causing the slow down.

Mia sped up as the directions led her to the county road. She passed under a canopy of trees, enjoying the open space of a single lane dirt road. Classic rock blared from the car speakers, giving voice to the angst she was feeling. The fuel needle was approaching empty but she could make it back to the interstate before needing a gas station.

A brilliant sky of purple and orange lay before her with no passing cars to distract. The change in scenery was helpful, but not enough to stop her from rethinking every word she said in the meeting. If she had just been more persuasive, maybe she could have won over the committee.

When ten minutes turned to fifteen, Mia began to doubt this shortcut. *Would it be that hard to give drivers a sign for what's ahead?* She glanced at her phone. The image on the screen was frozen. She tried to refresh it but had no cell reception.

The speedometer needle jumped from fifty to seventy miles per hour, a cloud of dust behind the Nova. If she was destined to be lost, at least she'd get there in record time. That was the secret to her survival. Stay busy. Make things happen. If you slow down, the world passes you by.

Several miles later, her car was running on fumes. Mia fluctuated between fear of running out of gas and anger at herself. She tried to calculate how much farther until the road merged back with the interstate. It couldn't be more than a few minutes, could it? Maybe she should turn around. She hated the thought of retracing the same miles. So inefficient. Besides, she didn't have enough gas to get all the way back anyway. Surely something was up ahead.

Mia shut off her phone and then restarted it, hoping to find a signal. Waiting. Waiting. Suddenly, the car jolted. Her phone fell to the floorboard. Then the engine locked. With no power, all she could do was force the steering wheel to the right and hope the car would coast to the side of the road before stopping.

She pounded her hand on the dash. How stupid to take an untested shortcut in an unknown area. Especially with so little gas in the tank. Shame covered her like a thick blanket. She picked up her phone. Still no service.

She had maybe an hour of sunlight before nightfall. The silence was disconcerting. No birds. No cars. And no point just sitting in her car. She got out and opened the trunk. She knew she wouldn't find a gas can but didn't know what else to do. A spare tire, a half-eaten bag of potato chips, and a pair of old running shoes were all that was back there. She traded her sandals for the running shoes and slammed the trunk.

She'd wait. Surely someone would drive by and see her stranded. She popped the hood and circled her car a few times. Then she sat on the trunk, her hair falling over her face, and tried to think of the best thing to do given the situation. Her mind was blank. Over the next hour, two cars passed without stopping.

That's it. I've got to do something or I'll be spending the night out here in the dark. She tossed the phone in her backpack, along with a jacket she had in the car, and slung it over her shoulder.

She walked down the road in the same direction she had been driving. If she only had an hour left of daylight, her hope rested in something up ahead. Not twenty miles behind her.

"I hate this!" she screamed. Her outburst was greeted by silence. "Why is everything always up to me?" She picked up a stone and threw it at the closest tree. She missed.

Mia shivered in the cool evening air. She put her jacket on and continued down the road. After a mile or so, she saw a sign up ahead. It was the first she'd seen since detouring down this county road. She jogged to it, her backpack hitting her lower back with each step. When she was close enough to read it, she stopped and laughed. The two faded words, Gas Ahead, looked like they'd been painted a decade ago. While it would've been nice to know *how* far ahead, the promise of fuel gave her the will to keep moving.

The walk left her with ample time to wrestle with thoughts she normally tried to avoid. Life wasn't working on any front and hadn't since she was a girl. Her father was the only one who'd ever believed in her. Until the day he drove off and never returned. She was only six years old and in the blink of an eye, her father simply was no more. Her mother raised her but never understood her.

She dug her phone from her pack. It was dead. There was no one to call anyway.

The last light of day gave way to a harvest moon and a smattering of stars that cast a surreal glow to the path. Mia's feet had blisters and her back ached from the overstuffed pack. *I should have stayed in my car. Or gone back the way I came. At least then I'd know what to expect.*

At first, she thought her eyes were playing tricks on her. But the closer she got, the more clearly she could discern the outline of a building. It was the gas station. She approached it and sighed. It wasn't just closed. It looked like it had been deserted years ago. She leaned against the rusted gas pump. So the sign promising help had been both right and not helpful.

She walked to the backside of the station. The door and windows were boarded up. But on the right side of the building was a metal bench.

Exhaustion overcame her. She let the pack drop from her shoulder and collapsed on the bench, with the reluctant acceptance that it was the safest place to rest for the night.

She took off her jacket and wadded it into a makeshift pillow. Unfamiliar sounds reminded her how far from home she was. Mia had no idea how to protect herself at an abandoned gas station in the middle of nowhere. If a wild animal chose to eat her, she just hoped it would be over fast. "I taste really bad," she announced to any nearby predator. "And I'm a chef, so I would know."

Her sarcasm provided little comfort. Mia looked up at the sky, her eyelids heavy. The flickering stars and full moon served as a ceiling. She felt small in such a vast universe. Thankfully, sleep came fast.

the shift
to with

THE ILLUSION OF CONTROL

Mia's dreams of becoming a chef seem all but dead. Strava passes on her for others with more potential. She's fired from her day job as a waitress. Her father was the only one who ever believed in her. He taught her to cook—and then disappeared from her life.

She has no money to pay the bills. She can't find her way home. And now she finds herself in the middle of nowhere. Out of gas . . . and out of hope.

When we feel the world closing in around us, it's easy to go into survival mode. We tighten our grip in an effort to not lose more. But what if we allow the unexpected and unwanted interruptions to remind us that we never were in control in the first place?

What if the disruptions we try so hard to avoid are actually opportunities in disguise? After all,

What if we allow the unexpected and unwanted interruptions to remind us that we never were in control in the first place?

the best part of a movie occurs when the hero's back is against the wall and all hope seems lost. Whether it's Indiana Jones surrounded by enemies on a rickety rope bridge or Doc Brown clinging to the clock tower in a lightning storm, our hearts beat faster as the emotions—and stakes—intensify.

But our lives aren't a movie. In the real world, interruptions seem less dramatic. The future of the world isn't in your hands. But a relationship is at stake. Setbacks are costly. And there are no guarantees. So when the unexpected happens, it seems safer to stabilize than step into the unknown.

But what if these disruptions are the gateway to a better life? Rather than trying to get things under control, what if you were to release the illusion of control? That feels risky. But doesn't it also feel enticing to consider letting go of what you were never meant to carry?

nightmares

A flutter of wings startled Mia from sleep. It was still night but something wasn't right. As her vision swam into focus, she remembered where she was . . . and screamed. A raven sat on the bench arm, its jet-black eyes staring at her.

"Shoo!" Mia jerked up and flung her arm at it.

The raven flew out of reach and landed on the ground. "Get off my bench."

Mia blinked her eyes in disbelief. "You... talk?" Her heart skipped a beat. This couldn't be. "I've got to wake up."

The raven pecked her leg.

"Ouch!"

"Still think this is a dream?"

The pain in her leg felt real enough. Mia tried to calm herself. "I'm asleep and I'm alone.

The raven mocked her. "Alone. All alone."

She kicked at the bird. "Get away from me, you stupid–"

"O'Neal."

"What?"

"My name. O'Neal." The raven turned his attention to a worm in the gravel. He tilted his head back and the worm slithered down his throat. Then he let out a high-pitched screech. Mia jumped as he spread his massive wings and flew into the air.

She stood, ready to swat the giant bird if it dove at her. But instead he began to circle her. As she watched the raven go around and around, Mia grew light-headed. The sky swirled before her. She closed her eyes so she wouldn't faint.

When she opened them, she was no longer at the gas station but in her girlhood home. Sunlight streamed through the open kitchen window. She gripped the mustard-colored counter top and took in the setting. What was going on?

Utensils, mixing bowls, and ingredients were scattered before her. This was her favorite room growing up. She'd learned the joy of cooking from her father. Even though he was no longer there, she most felt his presence whenever she was making something in the kitchen.

She looked at the creation before her and remembered. She'd just put the finishing touches on a cake she'd made from scratch. The peppermint frosting looked too good to resist. Mia ran a finger along the edge of the lopsided cake and then licked it. Delicious.

Her mother appeared in the kitchen, hair in a bun and hands on her hips. Immediately, Mia felt ten years old. And in that moment, she became her ten-year-old self.

"Mom, look what I made!" She cut a piece and handed the paper plate to her mom.

"What you made is a mess. Quit trying to be like your father and get this kitchen cleaned up."

"This was his favorite cake."

"He's not here anymore."

The young girl remained undeterred. "But he taught me how to make it. Will you at least take a bite?"

Her mom poked a finger at the pink dessert. "This looks like it came from a cheap box mix. Stop pretending you can cook like him. You're no cook. And stop acting like he's here. He's not and he's not coming back. You've got no father, Mia. Accept it."

Mia walked to the kitchen window to compose herself. When she turned around, she was alone. "Mom?"

She looked at the counter tops. Her mom was right, the kitchen was a mess. She took the bowls and measuring cups and placed them in the sink. Then she got the broom and swept the flour and sugar off the floor. When she opened the garbage can, she froze. Her mom's piece of cake lay on top, untouched.

Mia sighed. *She's right. I'm not a cook. And my dad isn't coming back.* Mia started to wipe down the counters when she saw movement across the room. O'Neal was perched on top of a chair at the kitchen table. She froze, held captive by the creature's relentless glare.

"What are you doing here?"

The bird cawed. Then repeated in a shrill imitation of her mother's voice, "No cook. No father."

As Mia stared in disbelief, the raven flew at her face. She squeezed her eyes shut and held her arms up to block the bird. When nothing happened, she opened her eyes. The kitchen had transformed into a school hallway. No longer a ten-year-old girl, she was a high school senior.

The abrupt shift in locations made her head throb. She leaned against a locker and closed her eyes. A bell rang and students poured from the doors into the long hall. She dreaded the walk between classes to her locker. It wasn't that the other kids mocked or bullied her. It's that no one paid her any attention at all. She'd try to start conversations, but no one heard her. If she missed class, no one noticed. She felt invisible.

She paused at a display case of school trophies. The mirror in the back of the case reflected the gold statues and the people behind her. But her own image was distorted. That's how she felt. Uncomfortable in her own skin. Not fully there, the real her never truly seen.

Mia kept moving. She made it to her locker and fumbled with the combination. Got it. The metal door flew open. She screamed as the raven burst out and darted through the hall, screeching. The other kids chatted with friends on their way to class, unaware what was going on around them.

The raven spread his wings and soared from side to side above the students' heads. He landed on top of the large wall clock, glaring at her.

Mia took off at a sprint in the opposite direction, determined to lose this foul creature. As she rounded the corner, she heard the rush of wings behind her. She ran into the first open door and slammed it behind her.

Breathing hard, she wiped sweat from her forehead. When she turned to see what room she was in, she gasped. It had happened again. She was out of the school and in her apartment. The coffee cup still half-full where she'd left it that morning.

She walked to the table where her checkbook and a stack of bills were spread out. Her stomach tensed at the thought of how to pay them with no money coming in now. A light breeze rustled the sheer curtains. She'd closed the window before she left.

She glanced at the kitchen clock. The hands had been ripped off and lay on the floor beneath it.

A black blur flew from the bedroom to the kitchen. The raven landed on the table, wings flapping, papers fluttering in the air. The corners of his beak stretched upward in a permanent grin.

"Remember."

"Remember what? Why are you doing this?" She was sick of being pursued by the feathered beast.

O'Neal wretched and a thick green fluid splashed onto the table. In it was the half digested worm he'd swallowed at the gas station.

"That's you, Mia."

She ran to the open window for fresh air. *I've got to get out of this nightmare.*

Flying to the ledge, O'Neal squawked, "Try to escape and bad things await."

Mia lunged at the raven and knocked him out the window. She slammed the pane shut before he could fly back in.

Looking out, she saw a mass of ravens in the sky. They hovered in place, resembling a black cloud. Except this cloud had hundreds of eyes staring at her. O'Neal joined them in their strange formation. *What were they doing?*

As one, they suddenly charged at the closed window. Mia backed up. They were coming too fast to put anything in front of the window. She ran to the opposite side of the room. It sounded like an explosion when the glass pane imploded. Shards sliced into her skin and shrieking birds swarmed through her apartment, slamming into walls and furniture.

Mia tripped over her coffee table. She tried to get up but the ravens descended on her. She curled into a ball as beaks yanked at her hair and talons dug into her flesh.

Before she lost consciousness, the image of pink cake in a trash can flashed through her mind. She felt the same. Abandoned by her dad. Unwanted by her mom. Unseen in high school. Discarded by Strava. And now scavengers picked her apart.

She was alone. And this is how it would end.

the shift
to with

WHEN FEAR TAKES FLIGHT

Notice how the events that shaped Mia as a girl are being used against her. The loss of her father. Her passion for cooking. The desire for her mother's approval. Her sense of being invisible in school. It's not just an attack on what she loves to do, it's a toxic interpretation of who she is—a woman all alone in this world.

Throughout the nightmare, her fears of being isolated, unseen, and out of time chase her. She runs, but they ultimately defeat her in what should be the safest place of all, her home.

The raven's warning is clear.

"Pursue your dreams and bad things await."

Deep down, our nightmares tell us the same. They try to hold us back from our dreams. *Life may not be what you hoped for,* our fears whisper, *but try to break free for something better and we will cut you to shreds.*

It seems counterintuitive, but what if the way to overcome your biggest nightmares is actually with even bigger dreams?

names

The smell of burning wood jarred Mia from her sleep. She was covered in sweat but relieved to be back at the gas station and free from the images that haunted her sleep.

As her eyes oriented to the bright fall morning, she stood and stretched. Her body was stiff from the unforgiving bench. She put her jacket on and grabbed her backpack. Best to keep moving. There would be no help here.

She started down the road, surprised by the chill in the air. Around the bend, a small plume of smoke swirled above the trees. As she got closer, she could hear the sound of wood popping and a voice singing softly. There, several yards off the path to her right, a man sat strumming his guitar by a campfire. His song was mesmerizing. She stood by the edge of the road, wondering what to do. Other than a few passing vehicles, this was the first person she'd seen since her car broke down.

The man stopped playing the guitar and stood. He had scraggly white hair and stooped. She could outrun him if she had to.

"Wasn't expecting company out here."

She waved as she walked across the overgrown grass where he had made camp. "I wasn't expecting to be here."

His coat was tattered and his eyes glassy. But within his unkempt beard, a smile overtook his wrinkled face. "What changed your mind?"

"My car ran out of gas. How close is the nearest station?"

He returned to the campfire. His head and his hands had a slight tremor. She wasn't sure if it was because of the cold weather or age.

"Depends which way you go."

This was getting her nowhere. "There's just this one road."

"It divides up ahead. Eat first. Then we'll talk."

"Do you have a phone I could borrow?"

"Just a guitar."

Mia rolled her eyes. *Alone in the woods and this is my knight in shining armor?* Yet, she was cold and the small fire beckoned her. And some food did sound good.

"Come on, have a seat."

She set her pack down next to his open duffel bag. Then moved to the far side of the campfire and sat across from him on an old log. "Where are you headed?"

"That bag's not for travelin'." He reached in and grabbed a handful of small white pieces of paper. "These are my name tags."

Mia walked to the duffel bag. "May I?" He nodded and she lifted the one nearest the top. It was the kind people wore at parties. HI, I AM _____. *Jim* was written in shaky handwriting on one. She pulled another out. *Thomas.*

"Are these names of people you've met here?"

He laughed. "Don't get any visitors out here. I write those names to try and remember my own. My memory is no good." He handed her a pen and a blank name tag. "You write your name there. That way I won't forget you."

"I'm Mia."

"I won't remember if you don't write it down. Go ahead, put it right there." He pointed with a trembling finger to the blank line.

She pondered what to write. "I am . . . lost."

He furrowed his brow.

"I've got plenty of other options. I am . . . out of gas. I am . . . losing my mind. Oh, here's one. I am . . . not worth hiring."

He swatted at her sarcasm. "That's how you feel. Not who you are."

She wrote *Mia* and stuck the tag on her jacket. She returned his pen.

"That's a pretty name." He smiled as he handed her an apple and a wedge of cheddar cheese. "Here's some energy for your journey. That pack looks heavy."

She glanced at her backpack sitting in the dirt. "It's filled with research I did for a job interview."

"To do what?"

"I'd love to be a chef at my own restaurant." She bit into the apple and swallowed.

"You'd make a great chef."

"I'm a long way from that dream. This interview was for an entry-level position at a big food company."

"Maybe that will —"

"I didn't get the job."

He scrunched his weathered face. "Give me your name tag." He pulled the pen from his pocket. "Hurry! I need to add a word before I forget."

She peeled the tag off her jacket and handed it to him. He scrawled the word *Chef* above her name.

She laughed. "If only it were that easy."

"Your face lit up when you spoke about your dreams. There's power in naming something before it happens, Chef Mia." Liquid sloshed from the cup in his shaking hand. Mia noticed the fire was starting to go out.

She unzipped her pack and pulled out a handful of papers. Mia tossed a few pages into the fire and watched as the flames grew in intensity.

The old man stared in wonder as the burnt pieces of paper drifted up and disintegrated into ash. "Some say your dreams turn into offerings when you let them go."

"That's a nice way of saying my dreams just went up in flames."

"No, not at all. Think of it as giving those dreams to the Creator." He offered a crooked smile. "I wonder what He'll do with them."

She threw more pages into the fire, not buying his naïve view of the world but thankful to release anything tied to Strava. They then sat in silence, enjoying each other's presence.

After a few minutes, she stood and slid one arm through her backpack strap. It hung from her left shoulder. "Thanks for the food. And for helping me lighten my load. Now which road should I take?"

He looked up with his glassy eyes. "I don't remember."

"But you said there's a split ahead."

"There is . . . but bad things await those who try to leave."

Mia froze. "Where did you hear that?"

"I told you I'm no good with names. Why do you ask?"

She was too embarrassed to say a talking raven. But it was almost word for word how O'Neal threatened her in the nightmare. She forced a smile. "No worries. It's not important."

But something else nagged at her. "If you never leave, where do you get your food?"

He pointed up with a shaky finger. "A friend takes care of my needs."

"Your food comes from the sky?"

He chuckled, revealing a missing tooth. "From a bird."

A shiver ran down her spine. "That makes no sense."

The old man looked at his watch. "He should be here any time now if you want to —"

She shook her head. "I've got to go." Mia wished she could take the kind soul with her, but he'd just slow her down. Or lead O'Neal to her. "When I find a gas station, I'll send help."

"This is my home. I don't need —" A seizure dropped the man to his knees. He grabbed his head as his body trembled uncontrollably. Mia rushed to his side.

He looked up, his eyes hazy. "Who . . . who are you?"

She hesitated. "You don't remember me?"

"My friend says not to talk to strangers. Please leave."

Mia took one step back as the man shuffled to the campfire and stoked the flames. If the

raven was real, then she was still in her nightmare. Or worse, awake in a world she no longer recognized.

the shift
to with

WHAT'S BEEN LOST

Like her old car, Mia finds herself out of gas and stuck in the middle of nowhere. She's slowly coming to grips with the fact that she's lost.

We all experience those moments. We lose sight of what matters most. We stop pursuing what brings us joy, and we slowly let go of the most important parts of our story.

Then we wake up one day and no longer recognize ourselves.

It's like wearing a blank name tag we hope others can fill in. We stay on this path until something or someone calls us to remember who we are.

Admitting we're lost is the first step to reclaiming our identity.

> It's like wearing a blank name tag we hope others can fill in. We stay on this path until something or someone calls us to remember who we are.

signs

She set her pack down at the split in the road. A brisk wind rustled the leaves at her feet. To call this a crossroads was an overstatement. Blink and you'd miss the thin path that veered from the main one.

Mia kept one eye on the sky since leaving the campfire man. Somehow the raven of her nightmare was haunting his days. Or the old man's memory was slipping further and this was part of his delusion. Maybe her mind was going as well.

At least he'd been right about the divide. She saw why he avoided it. Vines and branches caused it to blend with the forest floor. It sloped downhill. A forgotten, neglected path to nowhere.

But what caught her attention more was the sign fifty feet ahead on the main road. She walked to it. Shadow Hills – 7 Miles. Food, Gas, Lodging.

Bingo! That's the sign she'd been looking for. It was less than a quarter of a mile from his campfire. The old man was only seven miles from civilization and he'd never tried to get help? Or maybe he had and simply forgot because of his seizures.

Regardless, the sign brought Mia renewed hope. She would stay on the main road. She took a few steps forward, then remembered she'd left her pack at the crossroads. She sighed and went back. As she picked it up, she gave one last look to the path that veered into the woods. A reflection of sunlight in the brush caught her eye. *What is that?*

Intrigued, she set her pack down. Something shiny was hidden within the forest growth. As she stepped closer, she could tell it was several feet in length. Mia tugged at a thick veil of hanging vines. She snapped branches that had grown over and around the object. Underneath the foliage was metal, glass, and tires.

Nestled between trees and camouflaged under years of forest growth was an old truck that time had forgotten. She brushed the limbs and vines from the driver's door panel, noticing that the tires were flat.

This can't be.

Mia was staring at a rusty white truck. Though faded and cracked, a Franklin Farms logo was painted in red letters—the name of her dad's orchard. Her heart raced.

It was her father's truck. Twenty-three years after he disappeared, she stood next to his truck. She tripped on a vine as she walked to the passenger side. She pulled the branches from the door and yanked it open. The aroma of pipe smoke and cedar poured from the vehicle. Mia climbed into the cab and sat on the faded vinyl seat. The inside was smaller than she remembered.

Mia closed her eyes and let the scents take her back.

On their drives, she never sat in the passenger seat. She'd slide right next to him, her left arm and leg touching his as he drove.

The memory of one ride in particular swirled before her.

"Do you want to come with me, sweetheart? I need to—"

"Yes!"

Her dad smiled. "But you don't know where I'm going."

She grinned. "I don't care, Daddy."

"Then how do you know you want to go?"

"'Cause you're there."

"But what if I don't know the way?" her father asked with mock concern and a twinkle in his eyes.

Six-year-old Mia laughed. "You don't get lost, Daddy."

"What if I forget my wallet and we don't have money for ice cream?" he teased.

"You're being silly. You always have quarters in your pockets."

"We could run out of gas."

The young girl slapped him on the shoulder. "Who does that?"

"But what if the trip takes all day?"

She looked into his blue eyes. "Let's go, Daddy."

"That's my girl."

The memory faded, leaving her alone in the old truck.

The keys were gone. Not that the old vehicle would start now anyway. What was he doing here all those years ago?

His baseball cap and sunglasses sat on the dash, which was coated in a fine layer of dust. She held one, then the other. She could see him wearing both. She started to set them back on the dash, but then tossed the tangible reminders of her dad in her backpack.

Mia climbed out of the truck and wrestled the creaky door closed. She returned to where the path split. The sign before her promised all she had hoped for. But she just found a far more intriguing sign in the form of her father's truck.

She pulled her hair up into a handheld ponytail and took a deep breath. She looked down the neglected trail. Then she let go of her hair and grabbed her pack.

For some reason, her dad had chosen this path twenty-three years ago. It would be hers as well.

the shift
to with

INTO THE UNKNOWN

In the classic *Alice's Adventures in Wonderland*, the young girl finds herself before two paths. She asks the Cheshire Cat which way she should go.

"That depends a good deal on where you want to get to," said the Cat.

"I don't much care where–" said Alice.

"Then it doesn't matter which way you walk," said the Cat.

"–so long as I get *somewhere,*" Alice added as an explanation.

"Oh, you're sure to do that," said the Cat, "if you only walk long enough."[3]

3. Lewis Carroll, *Alice's Adventures in Wonderland* (United Kingdom, Macmillan, 1865).

Choices are like dominoes. Tip one over and it sets in motion an entire series of events. And they often fall in the most unexpected ways.

For miles, Mia had been waiting for a sign—something in the road offering tangible information on what was ahead. And it finally appeared. Then she found an even better sign. One that could lead Mia to her father.

One promises help and the return to normal life. The other has no guarantees. . . but holds the hint of something fantastical.

Easy and best are rarely on the same path.

You don't just want to get somewhere. You already know the meaninglessness of trying that approach.

> ## Easy and best are rarely on the same path.

Aiming for what's possible in your own strength sets the bar way too low. Why be limited by your current abilities? Simply achieving what's possible is, well, boring. Congratulations for doing what you already knew you could do. Yet we're often more comfortable deciding next steps based on our evaluation of options from a well-reasoned pros and cons list.

What if we instead pursued what the world calls impossible? God often draws us into places that lead to the end of our understanding.

At the crossroad, Mia trades the promise of food, gas, and shelter for the possibility of finding out what happened to her father.

Every hero's journey, including ours, reaches that moment when we either cling to the known or move into mystery. Both options involve risk and danger. But new pieces of the puzzle are only revealed as we brave the journey and step into the "not yet."

> Every hero's journey, including ours, reaches that moment where we either cling to the known or move into mystery.

Like Mia, we think we are looking for answers. We're actually searching for something far greater . . . our true home.

invitation

She hated walking away from her dad's truck. It felt like she was losing him all over again.

Yet she knew whatever answers there were would be ahead, not behind her.

Over several miles, the trail gradually leveled. Under different circumstances, Mia would have savored the beauty of the autumn woods. But she was desperate to untangle what happened to her father–then get back to her apartment with running water and a warm bed.

She rounded a bend and came to an abrupt stop. Off the road to her right several yards ahead was a stone house. A wooden barn and stable sat behind it. Mia picked up her pace.

She was breathing hard as she stepped onto the front porch and knocked on the oak door. A moment later, she tried again, then decided to walk around to the back of the house. As she turned the corner she saw a barefoot woman in faded jeans and a beaded white shirt heading her way. She was holding a pair of leather riding boots, wet mud squishing between her toes as she walked. Her silver hair was in a ponytail, swaying side to side.

"Morning."

"I don't mean to trespass. My car broke down and I was wondering if I could borrow your phone."

"You're most welcome here, Mia. I'm Iona."

"How do you know my name?"

Iona's deep blue eyes danced with joy. "Your name tag, Chef Mia."

She looked down and grinned sheepishly. "My friend has a thing about names. If I could just use your phone, I'll be out of here in no time."

A rustic wood table in the backyard was set with food and drink. "Wait here. I'll be right back," Iona said before heading inside her home.

Mia stood at the table and admired the rolling hills that bordered Iona's land. Several yards away was her barn with a paddock and stables. The setting was idyllic, but she was more interested in what was right in front of her.

On the table was a bowl of raspberries, a plank of grilled salmon, a tray of baked sweet potatoes, and a cutting board with warm bread and butter. She took the pitcher of ice water with orange slices and poured herself a glass. Small candles were lit and sat in pools of melted wax on the table.

In one long swig, Mia drank the entire glass of water. She ran her hand across the table's uneven surface. She was about to sample the berries when Iona reappeared.

"Here's the phone. Feel free to make your call. But I hope you'll join me for lunch first." Iona went to the bread and began slicing a piece for each of them.

"This is quite a spread. You must be expecting company."

Iona buttered the bread and then handed it to Mia. "Actually, I was anticipating your arrival."

Mia took the bread and smelled it, a slight smile on her face. "That's impossible."

"As you'll see, very little is impossible here."

Mia thought about her cryptic response as she took a bite of bread. It was delicious. "But I didn't even know I would be coming this way."

"Then your timing is excellent." Iona said as she sat in the chair across from Mia. "Please, let's begin while the food is warm."

She was too hungry to resist. She sat and scooped generous portions of everything into her plate. Iona made herself a salad with wild berries, pine nuts, and kale. Mia tried to pace herself, but devoured everything on her plate and went for seconds. As she ate, Mia kept one eye on the birds in the redwood trees near them.

"Are there ravens around here?" Mia paused in her eating to refill her water glass.

Iona raised an eyebrow.

"Never mind. It's complicated."

"We sometimes make things more complicated than they need to be." Iona smiled and looked Mia in the eye. "Why did you take this path? It's not exactly the road most traveled."

"I planned to take the main road until—" Mia wasn't sure how to finish her sentence. "Until something changed my mind."

"What would that be?" Iona took a bite of her salad.

"My father's truck. He's been gone more than twenty years and I find it here in the middle of nowhere."

Iona stopped chewing.

"I know, right? It makes no sense. It sounds pretty complicated to me. So I appreciate your hospitality but I just need to find a gas station and get back to my car."

"What about your father's truck?"

"I can't even process that yet. Maybe I'll have it towed once I get my car up and running."

Iona slid her phone to Mia. "The number's on the screen. The shop is less than ten miles away."

Mia dialed. A loud voice shouted over a revving engine, "Hello. Ted's Garage."

"Is this Ted?"

"It's his brother Ned. How can I help you?"

"Ned, my car ran out of gas near the interstate. I need—"

"Hold on. Let me get my brother Ed." *Ted, Ned, and Ed. Mia grinned, wondering how a mother could do that to her sons.*

Iona fidgeted, moving a few items on the table.

"Ma'am, this is Ed. Okay, we can—"

Iona waved a hand at her.

"Ed, just a second." Mia put her hand over the receiver. "What?"

Iona bit her lower lip. "We need to talk"

"Fine, after I finish this we—"

"No, Mia. Now."

She went back to the call. "Ed? Thanks for holding. You were saying?"

Iona reached over and gently put her hand on Mia's arm. "Your father. He was here at this table."

Mia dropped the phone and stared at Iona in disbelief.

She twirled a strand of silver hair from her ponytail and lowered her eyes. "He arrived at my door many years ago. Said his truck had broken down. So I helped him."

"But his truck is still there."

"He didn't need a truck where he was going."

"What are you talking about? What happened to my father?"

Iona clasped her hands together. "I can't fully say."

"You can't or you won't?"

"I can tell you what he was looking for."

Mia stood and ran her fingers over her forehead and through her hair. "How would you know that?"

"He was desperate for a better way to live. He was more broken down than his truck. His life was unraveling on numerous fronts."

"That's not true."

"Mia, you were just a girl then. You wouldn't have known."

"So what did you do?"

"I told him about a place that offers hope."

"What does that mean? Where did he go?"

"Please sit down, Mia. This will take some time to explain."

She hesitated for a moment, then exhaled loudly and joined Iona at the table.

"Let me ask you a question. Do you ever feel like you don't quite belong here?"

"Here?"

"In the world around you."

"We're talking about my dad, not me."

"I'm talking about something that affects both of you. I know this seems like a rabbit trail. But it is not. Do you ever feel alone, even in a group of people? Like something is missing but you can't quite say what? Do your dreams seem like they are always out of reach...or even opposed?"

Mia didn't respond but her eyes gave her away.

"That's what brought your father here. And now you."

She sighed. "I've always felt like an outcast. Like I don't fit in anywhere."

"What if it's the surroundings that don't fit you?" Iona asked. "I know this sounds bizarre, but two very different atmospheres exist in this world. Your father was suffocating in the one he lived in. He had heard rumors of another place. I confirmed them."

"You're as crazy as the old man in the forest. There aren't two worlds."

"Not two worlds. Two ways to exist in the world. Your feelings of being overwhelmed and not enough? It's what you were born into. Not where you have to stay."

"You're asking me to go somewhere different?"

"The invitation is to become someone different. The atmosphere changes when you change."

Mia stood up and crossed her arms. "Where is my dad?"

"His journey was . . ." Iona's voice faded.

"You're full of answers until it comes to him."

"Perhaps you value answers too much."

Mia raised her palms "All you do is talk in riddles. I didn't ask for any of this. I just got lost on my way home."

Iona stood before her, the wind blowing her ponytail. "You've been lost a long time, Mia. The choice is whether or not you want to be found."

She looked down at the phone. Then back at Iona. "If you can help me find my dad, I'm in. But you have to promise me that."

"Mia, I understand your desire for guarantees. But you must focus on your own Story before you can help another."

"That's not good enough. I'm done here." She reached for the phone.

Iona put her hand over Mia's. "Why not stay through the meal? Let me tell you more. Then decide."

Mia wanted to run away, but the hope of finding her father kept her from moving. She turned and faced Iona. "All right, keep talking. Tell me why I should trust anything you say."

$$\dfrac{the\ shift}{to\ with}\longrightarrow$$

THE ORPHAN REALM

Sometimes the best we can do is simply stay present when we want to turn and run. That's all Mia can do in the moment. But it is enough.

If what Iona says is true about the existence of two atmospheres, that may explain where her father is. And if he can get there, maybe she can too. Any place would be better than her current reality—where her dreams have been denied and her heart numbed from constant disappointment.

When you're stuck in the Orphan Realm, you believe you're alone and that life is totally up to you. It describes how you approach life—and the state of your heart. That's why it's possible to live from this place even if you're surrounded by a loving family or have numerous friends.

In this realm, a person's worth is based on what he or she does. How you perform is what matters.

You don't automatically have a place at the table. You earn it every day. After all, God gave you a mind and a body. Now get busy and make things happen. Because it is all up to you. If you fail, you are a failure. If you succeed, you are a performer who needs to produce even more next time. You can't even unplug for an occasional vacation, because if you aren't reachable then you may become disposable.

These beliefs run so deep. It's as if they are tattooed on our souls. Outwardly, we appear to have it all together. But inwardly, we are weary and running on fumes. Fear and worry keep us going, but where exactly are we headed?

Does this describe your reality?

Striving and control are key traits of those in this realm. That was me. Remember my fortune cookie message? No matter what success I achieved, there was little joy. Instead, I was wiped out yet knew I had to gear up for the next mission impossible.

When resources are scarce, someone has to win and someone has to lose. Another person's victory is hard to celebrate when it is interpreted as your loss. So you try to control the details and people around you. Not only does this not work, it is exhausting. Which increases the sense of being overwhelmed, alone, disheartened, and diminished.

Notice, too, that the dreams of those in this realm are constantly under attack. Some are told they don't yet have enough experience to pursue their ideas. They are too young or haven't paid

> Another person's victory is hard to celebrate when it is interpreted as your loss.

their dues yet. Ironically, others are told they are too old and that their time has passed. In either case, the message is the same. Time isn't on your side. You don't have enough of it...or you're running out of it.

Iona hasn't said much about the second realm yet. At this point, all we know is that a better place exists.

Mia is skeptical. She's not ready to open her mind or heart to the possibility of something so fantastical. She'd walk away except this woman might hold the key to finding her father.

Iona knows more information won't break the fog of Mia's current reality. So she decides to proceed with something more disruptive than facts—a story.

brownstone

Iona began to stack the dishes on the table. She set aside the leftover bread, tearing it into smaller pieces for the birds. "Maybe I should tell you more about me. Some people are teachers. Some are architects. I am a Guardian. I help travelers escape the chains of this reality and enter into a place of freedom."

"What are you saying?"

"I offer people a chance to see their Story in a new way. This home was built on what some refer to as a thin place. From here, I usher the hungry into a place where their souls can be fed."

"And people just appear on your doorstep?"

"Like you have, yes. When they are ready."

"But how does—"

"Mia, this is not something I can fully explain in the time we have. There is an enemy who will do anything to stop travelers from finding freedom. He is likely quite close."

Mia thought about the raven and shivered. Iona's words stirred an uneasy mix of hope and fear within her.

"So let me get this straight. You're telling me there's some place where I can be free of all the things that hold me back. And you can help me get there?"

Iona nodded.

"And this is what my dad agreed to?"

"That's correct."

"But then you lost track of him."

Iona poured another glass of water from the pitcher. "As a Guardian, I help people experience new ways to live. But I don't know what will happen once their Stories begin. I've not been given that power."

Mia wondered what power Iona had been given. "So how do I get to this other place?"

"Through the Blue Door."

Mia rolled her eyes. "Come on. I want to find my dad and the best you can offer is a magical door?"

Iona raised an eyebrow. "You thought the Blue Door was legend?"

Mia smirked. "I've never even heard of the blue door. Please don't tell me this trip involves pixie dust, rainbows, and unicorns."

"Pixie dust? That's ridiculous." She took a sip of the cool water. "But there is a Blue Door. It's the entry to your true home."

"And this supposed door—" Mia looked out over the rolling hills and admired the color of the changing leaves. "Does it happen to be here in the forest?"

"You're jumping ahead. You must be ready for the Blue Door before you can enter it. That's why we begin with Story."

"I'm not really into stories. Can we just cut to the chase? I'm a fast learner."

"You're correct. You've learned the ways of your realm incredibly well. Now it's time to unlearn them."

Mia sat in silence, the phone on the table next to her. She wanted to leave and never look back. It all sounded so impossible. But her entire life had been practical and predictable. And that hadn't led her to her father...or anything but disappointment.

"All right, tell me the story."

"The Story has yet to be written. I can't tell it. But I can take you there."

"So you're coming with me?"

"I can get you there. That is all I can promise."

A sudden breeze caused the candle flames to flicker. There was a chill in the air. Iona's expression turned more serious. "The enemy nears. We must begin the Story now. Give me your hands."

Feeling a bit foolish, Mia reached across the table and took Iona's hands. The air around her began to ripple in waves. She started to feel dizzy so she closed her eyes.

Iona's voice slowed and took on a more serious tone. "There was once a girl who loved to dream. But as she grew, her dreams didn't come true. She loved her father. But was told he was gone forever. So she shut that part of her heart down and decided life was up to her. That she was alone . . . an orphan."

Eyes shut, Mia nodded in agreement.

"That Story is a lie." As Iona spoke those words, the atmosphere shifted. Mia grew light-headed. It felt as if the ground opened and she was spiraling downward.

"We now enter into a place where ideas take on shape and form. Where the impossible is possible. And where we have eyes to see a truer Story. "

Though she was sure they remained in the forest, Mia now could hear the clinking of glasses and the hiss of an espresso machine. "I smell coffee."

"Open your eyes, Mia."

They sat at a metal table with two steaming cups of coffee before them. Mia jerked her hands away. "What's going on? Is this the other place?"

"No, we are in Story."

"Looks like a coffee shop to me."

"How do you think a Story is supposed to look? This coffee shop is in the basement of an old brownstone building. That's where this part of your Story begins."

"I get it. I'm really in the forest but I'm seeing the story you're telling . . . like a vision or dream?"

"You dream when you are asleep. Story requires you to be fully awake. And Mia, the consequences here last longer than any dream."

"But none of this is real, right?"

"It depends what you mean by real."

Mia looked around them. "Where is my backpack?"

"It's not needed for your journey." Iona reached into her jacket and handed Mia a small brown leather pouch tied with rope. "But this is."

Mia untied the string at the top and set the pouch on the table. Within were four glass vials, in two rows of two. They were held in place by thin velvet straps. She lifted them out one at a time. Each was a unique shape and color with words carved into the glass.

One was blood-red with a heart etched into it. The word *Awaken* was inscribed along the side. The one that appeared to be the oldest had a pearl-like finish. On it was the word *Together*. Another was a deep blue and had *Identity* carved into it. The last was a seafoam-green color and resembled the kind of bottle you'd put a note in and cast to the sea. Except it was no larger than a test tube. She ran her fingers over the word on that vial. *Expectant*. Each was sealed with a cork, even though the vials were empty.

Mia looked at Iona. "What am I supposed to do with these?"

"You need them for your journey. Keep them in the pouch for now."

Mia gave the vials one last look, then put them in the leather pouch and slipped it into her jacket pocket.

Iona reached across the table and took hold of Mia's hands. "You can't return as long as the vials remain empty."

"Wait. Return from where?"

"Why, the Story of course." Iona brushed a strand of silver hair from her face.

"What goes in them?"

"Whatever each requires. A vial must be filled at every level. Satisfy it and you move forward. Don't . . . and you don't."

"Say things go wrong. Can you get me out?"

"If you quit, you won't make it out of the Story." Iona's eyes darted to the tables around them. "I need to leave before the enemy senses my presence here."

"The enemy is here? How do I stay safe?"

"You'll have help."

Mia took a deep breath, trying to reassure herself. "I'll be fine. I mean, this is a Story, not a matter of life and death."

Iona held her ceramic coffee mug in front

of Mia, then let it drop. It shattered on the tile floor, hot coffee splashing their shoes and the base of the table. The people at tables near them stared for a moment, then went back to their conversations.

Iona picked up a piece of ceramic from the floor. She pricked her finger with it. A thin line of blood appeared.

"Are you insane?"

"What happens here is real, Mia. Get cut, you bleed. Get killed, you die."

"You're dropping me into a story that you just *hope* I make it out of?"

"My hope is that this Story will prepare you for what is ahead." Iona pressed a napkin on the cut to stop the bleeding. "Listen carefully. We're in the basement of a six-story brownstone. There are five levels above us. You must go to the elevator in the lobby and take it to the first floor."

"An elevator? I thought I was looking for a blue door."

"First you must find the elevator. Once you get to the first floor, you'll need the vials for passage to each of the next levels. And Mia . . . the sequence matters. You must successfully complete each level. Do not attempt to bypass a floor."

"Sure. Hit every floor. Got it. But I have four vials and you said there are five levels above the basement."

"You have all you need. It's time to go."

Mia saw a door leading from the coffee shop to the lobby. When she turned back, she was alone at the table.

"Great. Don't bother saying bye," Mia mumbled. "I'll be just fine." Then she thought of Iona's warning about the enemy. "Or maybe I'll die. Here's hoping this story isn't a tragedy."

Iona had left cash on the table for their drinks. Mia walked from the coffee shop to the lobby. The old bricks and architectural style of the brownstone seemed from another century. People paid her no attention. When she reached the elevator in the center of the lobby, Mia pushed the Up button.

The metal door whisked open. Inside, the elevator was paneled in dark wood with six antique cream-colored ceramic buttons on the control panel. Thankful that no one else needed a ride, she pushed the button with 1 on it. The door slid shut. A computer voice announced, "First floor. Going up."

Mia took a deep breath. *Okay, I can do this. Whatever is on the next floor, I can handle it.*

The elevator dinged and slowed to a stop. She stepped back, straightened her jacket, and cleared her throat.

When the door opened, a massive wall of water swept Mia off her feet. In seconds, it completely filled the small space. Mia tumbled underwater, trying to determine which way was up. She was running out of air. With dread, she realized she was about to drown in an elevator.

the shift
to with

STEPPING INTO STORY

Mia has entered into Story. And quickly finds herself in over her head.

Some stories offer a way to unplug from reality. Yet the better stories usher us into a deeper reality. These kinds of stories rip a seam in the atmosphere so that the unseen starts to become visible. Think of it as a portal that provides a glimpse of God and His kingdom. Much like the parables of Jesus did.

Iona knew that kind of story was the only way for Mia to awaken to a new way of being.

> Some stories offer a way to unplug from reality. Yet the better stories usher us into a deeper reality.

The key is to remember that our life is a story. It is not a page of polished dates and facts, laid out like a resume, but a series of unexpected twists, deep emotion, unspeakable tragedy, and beautiful triumphs.

There are no do-overs or jumping ahead. We must simply live each moment as it comes.

Iona has given Mia few hints as to what's coming next. The four vials offer some clue to her mission. She knows she must stop at each level of the brownstone. She hopes to see her father. And she's been warned she'll encounter both an enemy and an ally on this journey.

We have no more prep when we step into our Story most mornings. The only question is whether we're looking for our Father as intently as Mia along the way.

waves

Her lungs burned and her head pounded under the pressure. She saw a glimmer of light to her left and propelled herself toward it.

Breaking the water's surface, she gulped deep breaths of air. Mia dog-paddled to stay afloat, but knew her strength would soon fade.

The elevator and the brownstone had somehow been washed away. She was in the ocean. This couldn't be possible. Not in the real world. But in this story . . . well, she wasn't sure.

Her arms and legs burned from constant motion. Mia recalled Iona's words that whatever happened in Story had real consequences.

If she went under, would she die here and vanish from the real world? That wasn't a helpful thought. She had to stay afloat.

"I'm coming!" a male voice cried out.

"Help!" She couldn't see anyone over the sloshing waves or the glare off the water. Every attempt to take a breath resulted in a mouthful of water. Her body gave out and she began to sink.

Mia felt herself slipping down in the cool water. Suddenly a strong arm wrapped around her waist and pulled her up. She was placed on a hard surface. She opened her eyes just long enough to see she was no longer under water . . .

She awoke to the rhythmic sound of waves and a salty breeze. The screech of a sea gull pierced the air.

"Where are we?" Her throat ached.

"On a paddleboard."

She raised her head slightly. She was horizontal on a six-foot paddleboard, her hands hanging over in the water. "No—*where* are we?" She shivered even though the sun warmed her body.

"The Pacific Ocean."

She turned to her rescuer. Only his head and shoulders were above the water. The muscular young man held the side of his board with one hand. A paddle was in the other. He had dark eyes and a darker tan.

"I'm Mia." She coughed up water. "I don't surf."

He grinned. "I pretty much guessed that. My name is Shay. How did you get out here?"

Mia wiped her hair away from her face. "Long story."

"What's the short version?"

"I was in an elevator. The door opened, a tidal wave crashed in, and I surfaced here."

Shay's brow creased. "That's, um, interesting. Listen, Mia, why don't you rest a few minutes. Then I'll get us to shore."

She squinted, trying to see land. The sun reflecting off the surface made it impossible and the salt water stung her eyes. "How far out are we?"

"Maybe fifteen minutes if we catch some good waves. I just need you strong enough to sit on your knees and stay balanced while I paddle us in." They bobbed up and down on the gentle waves, Shay still in the water.

"I've never been in the ocean before. I prefer heated pools."

"You won't catch any waves in a pool." Shay scanned the horizon as he spoke.

Mia licked her dry lips, tasting salt. "Maybe not, but I won't drown there either."

Shay laughed. "You know why the water's always warm in the kiddy pool, right?"

Mia grimaced. "There is that downside."

He seemed to study her. "I'm glad I was waiting on a wave or I wouldn't have seen you go under."

"Waiting drives me crazy."

Shay laughed. "Actually, I wait more than I ride. I want the right wave. Not just the next one."

"Waves all look the same to me."

Shay grinned. "Do me a favor. Slap some water my way. Come on, give it your best shot."

She leaned over and splashed Shay. "There. Happy?"

"Not really. I can't ride that one. Guess all waves aren't the same, huh?"

Mia felt her strength returning. "I think I'm good to go, you know, whenever the right waves are ready."

Shay helped Mia sit on the board. "How's that feel?"

The board shifted in the water, but Mia kept her balance. "I'm okay."

"Good. Now I need you to get on your knees near the back of the board." Once Mia was set, Shay went from being in the water to standing on the board in one fluid motion. The paddle was in his right hand.

He gave her a thumbs-up but then just stood at the front of the board, watching.

"We're not doing anything."

"We are." Shay pointed behind them. "See that swell starting to build?"

Mia turned. "Barely. What do we do?"

"We wait. If it's the right wave, I'll use my paddle to take us in."

What looked to be the start of a wave played out and was absorbed back into the ocean.

"Well that was disappointing," Mia said.

"Only if you expected it to be more."

"I don't get it. Isn't that the reason we're waiting?"

"We wait in anticipation. Not expectation."

Mia tried to simply be present. On her knees, she took in the water below and the sky above. Shay stood like a sentinel in front of her, paddle in his right hand, his eyes studying the rhythm of the ocean. He somehow was both ready and at rest.

"Look," he pointed to a rise that was starting to build several yards out. He placed the tip of the paddle to the surface of the water. The board swayed as the cresting wave neared.

"You can do this, Mia!"

Her heart beat faster as the wave approached. It propelled the paddleboard forward in a surge of motion.

Shay whooped. "Let's ride this!" He used the paddle to keep them pointed toward land but let the water do the work. Wave upon wave followed. Mia enjoyed the cool mist on her face as they coasted closer to shore. Then the waves subsided.

"I think we can touch bottom now." Shay jumped off the board. Mia shifted from her knees to a sitting position and then slid off into the waist-deep water. It felt good to have the ocean floor beneath her. They waded the rest of the way in.

When they got to the shore, Mia collapsed onto the warm sand. Her clothes were soaking wet, but she had nothing to change into. Shay placed the paddle on his board and sat next to her.

Arms propped behind her, Mia enjoyed the ocean view from the safety of land.

"Thanks for saving me out there."

Shay nodded. "It's all good, Mia." Then, like a shaggy dog, Shay shook his thick hair and sprayed her with water.

"Hey!" she laughed.

"Did the ride in wear you out?"

"No, that was actually invigorating. But I am tired of trying to make my own waves."

"In the ocean?"

"In life."

He nodded. "If we let it, waiting puts us in a place of childlike wonder. It's staying expectant for what's to come without striving to make something happen."

Expectant. The word jarred Mia back to her mission. She unzipped her jacket pocket and took out the leather pouch. She then laid each of the vials gently on the sand.

"What are those?"

"Vials. They're what helps me move forward on this journey."

"Where are you headed?"

"To find my father."

"Empty containers can help you do that?"

"I hope so. I need to fill each with the right element."

"How do you know which vial to start with?"

"You made that part easy. Each has a word etched into the side." She found the one labeled *Expectant*.

She held the seafoam-green vial up to Shay, as if she were giving a toast. "To being expectant!"

Shay smiled. "Hey, where's my glass?"

Mia carefully placed the other three containers into the pouch and back into her jacket. She slid the Expectant vial into the front pocket of her wet jeans.

Shay stood and dusted sand from his hands. "I don't know what kind of journey you're on, but it's awesome that it started with the ocean. And man, I get why being expectant comes first. It's hard to enter what's best if you're fearing the worst . . . or just more of the same."

Mia grinned. "Can I borrow your paddle-board?"

He fist-pumped the air. "I knew you'd want more!"

She waded into the water with the board and paddle. When Mia could no longer touch the ocean floor, she climbed on the board and sat on her knees. The paddle rested on her lap. She was content to simply be in the water.

Shay watched from the shore, his head cocked to the side. For a surfer who likely had seen it all, he seemed genuinely curious about what would come next.

She held the open vial. Then she waited. Not impatiently but expectantly. There were no waves in sight. She felt the motion of the water and sensed she should move a bit farther out and to her right. She did and then enjoyed floating. Mia savored the wind, the sun, and the sounds of the ocean. After several minutes, the water twenty yards out began to churn. She paddled a bit more to the right. Could it be that rather than having to make waves, the waves were actually made for her? That her role was simply to stay expectant?

As the wave rose, she tilted the vial toward the oncoming water. It surrounded her in cool wet comfort. Mia closed her eyes as the paddleboard surged forward.

The next thing she knew, she was sitting on the elevator floor. Her clothes were soaking wet. And in her left hand was a vial filled with ocean water. She had made it through the first level.

the shift
to with

STAY WITH GOD

There is an ocean of difference between expectations and expectancy.

Expectations indicate a sense of what should be. It is how we expect things to go, often veering into entitlement. If circumstances don't go the way we want, we feel cheated, irritated, or even offended. It's not fair. Change—especially change we didn't ask for—is viewed as an interruption to our plans. Many of us have carried unmet expectations for years that we need to let go of. Doing so will release these toxic emotions over something we never should have counted on to begin with.

Staying expectant is the opposite. It reflects anticipation for what's to come. It is being open to what *does* happen regardless of what you think *should* happen. Life is not meant to be something we control but something we experience.

There will be times when things go from bad to worse. In those moments, the pull to fear or worry is hard to overcome. It almost feels right to express those emotions. But when we look to God rather than our own strength or understanding, we experience something different: expectancy. That doesn't mean we accept the situation passively. Or pretend everything is sunshine and roses. Not at all. But we step into it with God. This requires the humility to accept the fact that we don't know how things will ultimately work out. Thankfully, the future isn't constrained to our list of potential outcomes. Where we see looming problems and limited options, He sees an exponential range of possibilities.

It's impossible to be expectant and controlling at the same time. Our hands—and our hearts— are either open or closed. One is a posture of relinquishing control. The other is a posture that grows more rigid.

Whenever I grow impatient, or think I know best and forge ahead from my own strength, the results are never optimal. It initially may feel good. Hey, at least I'm doing something. But later, when things go wrong or my actions led to unexpected consequences, I begin to doubt if I made the right decision.

I realize that if I can accomplish something purely in my own strength, those dreams were way too small.

But when I stay with Him no matter what I face, it gives me an unshakeable peace about the decision. Because it was made with God . . . in His timing. That's easier said than done. But He draws us into

> I realize that if I can accomplish something purely in my own strength, those dreams were way too small.

the deep to make us deeper. The shallow stunts our ability to learn to ride bigger waves. That's why God continually calls His sons and daughters to graduate from the baby pool and be wave riders in uncharted water. The kind we can only navigate with Him.

The Expectant vial is required at the first level of Mia's journey because she is entering a Story unlike any she has experienced. She is literally in over her head. The only possible way forward is to stay with God . . . actively waiting and expectant for the waves He will provide.

ingredients

Mia paced in the elevator, water dripping from her shivering body as she tried to process what just happened. *Okay, so I'm in a place where an elevator can open to an ocean, and a vial filled with the right substance can bring me back.*

The small space made her claustrophobic. She opened the pouch, slid the Expectant vial back into it, and then pushed 2 on the control panel.

"Level 1 complete. Going up." The digitized voice startled her.

Literally anything could be on the other side of the elevator door at the next three levels.

If it's up to me, I'm toast. But it isn't. I choose to stay expectant . . . and stay with the Creator. And I will find my dad. Mia pressed her back against the handrail on the far wall, putting as much distance as possible between her and the metal door.

It opened to the scent of fresh baked bread and warm cinnamon. Sounds of clanging utensils and robust laughter filled the air. It appeared to be the entrance to a large Italian kitchen.

The elevator door started to close, so Mia quickly stepped out.

Handwritten in chalk on a blackboard to her left were the words *Cook Wild. Feast Well.* She took a deep breath. She thought back to the rules posted at the Strava test kitchen. They brought stress where these four words awakened her heart.

She walked under the brick arc into a kitchen bustling with activity. Chefs rolled out dough and placed flatbread pizzas in large ovens. Others stirred vats of what appeared to be red and white frosting. A woman in a white smock raced by carrying several dozen eggs in a large glass bowl. The smell of fresh-baked cinnamon streusel caused Mia's stomach to growl.

"I need more citrus zest!" a voice shouted.

"On it!" another responded.

Behind her, a man cleared his throat in an exaggerated manner. Mia turned but didn't see anyone.

"Madame."

She dropped her gaze. A robust man stood before her, hands on his hips. He couldn't have been more than five feet tall but his dark beard and huge chef's hat amplified his presence. Mia nervously swallowed, unsure what to say.

"Where's your apron?"

"But I . . ."

"Come. You are here to cook, not look."

"You want me...to cook here?"

He enjoyed a hearty laugh. "You are in flavor town. Why else would you be here?"

The cooking area was expansive with various stations. Chefs were moving with a spring in their steps, humming as they focused on their works of art.

"I love to cook. What's all this food being prepared for?"

"It looks delicious, no?" He pinched two fingers together, raised them to his lips, and then released it as a kiss. "We are creating a feast for a large gathering tonight." He looked at the small puddle of water around her feet and frowned. "Madame, you are dripping wet."

"That's from the ocean on the first floor."

His bushy eyebrows lifted. He opened his mouth to say something, then closed it.

"I know it sounds crazy. You can thank Iona for that."

"Iona?" His entire face broke into a large grin and he spread his arms. "If you are friends with Iona, you are welcome here. She is the very one we're making this feast for. I am Chef Gino."

She shook his hand firmly. "I'm Mia."

"You mentioned your love of cooking. Are you a chef?"

"I used to be."

"Used to be? You find yourself here of all places, in the best kitchen in the world. Do you think that coincidence?" He grabbed an apron from a cubby next to him. "Here, put this on. You will be a chef again."

"What do you want me to make?"

"What do you desire?"

Mia blinked, unsure what he meant. "I'm sorry. What?"

"Choose what you are drawn to!" The stocky chef pointed toward the enormous pantry. "Select seven ingredients and meet me back here."

She looked at the pantry but hesitated.

He offered a gentle smile. "What do you hunger for, Mia?"

"I . . . don't know. I've never been asked that before. I just know how to follow recipes."

He cringed. "Recipes reflect another's creation." He spread his stubby arms wide. "Go to the pantry and see what ingredients stir your senses. You entered my kitchen a recipe follower but will leave a bohemian cook."

The contrast between this and Strava's test kitchen couldn't be greater. A place of doing versus a place of discovery. "So any seven ingredients, right?"

"Yes. But don't think of the dish. Let your desire lead you. The most essential ingredient is your imagination."

The pantry was the size of a small restaurant. She scanned the items on the massive oak shelves. Green peppers, red onions, and wild mushrooms sat next to prime cuts of meat and a scandalous assortment of cheeses.

She picked up a small metal basket. "Okay, what is speaking to me?" She'd never approached cooking this way before. It felt awkward . . . and freeing. She placed a pound of lean beef tenderloin wrapped in white butcher paper into the basket. She followed that with a slab of pale yellow Gruyère cheese, pungent arugula, a vine-ripened tomato, some fresh jalapeño, and a ripe avocado. A jar of honey reminded her of times at her grandfather's farm. She added it as well.

Chef Gino was waiting when she came out of the pantry. His arms were full of shiny utensils.

"I got the items I was drawn to."

"Always the best place to start." Chef Gino beamed. "Now let's see why these items wanted to come together." He led her to a preparation area. "This kitchen is our playground. We create from ingredients that make us smile. And we do it together, helping each other shape ideas into feasts."

Two chefs, a man and woman, stood at an enormous granite countertop. The man's forearms were covered in Celtic tattoos. The woman wore a bandana and was sharpening knives with amazing speed and precision.

The kitchen was surrounded in floor-to-ceiling windows. The view outside was a snow-capped mountain range.

"Fellow chefs, meet Mia. Let us show her the bohemian way to create."

She gave her basket of ingredients a nervous glance. "I have no idea what this will make."

"We follow your lead, Mia," the Celtic Chef said.

The woman in the bandana flashed a grin. "That's true, girl. But we'll work together to help this become *your* creation."

Mia closed her eyes and smiled. "Something sizzling sounds good. Maybe a hot sandwich?"

"Let us begin!" Chef Gino announced.

As Mia took the ingredients out of the basket, Bandana slapped the counter. "Honey is sweet. The jalapeño adds heat. That's good taste tension. I'll make a honey infusion."

Mia's shoulders slumped. "I forgot bread."

"How could you have chosen it before it was available?" Chef Celtic bent over the oven and pulled out a loaf of hot focaccia bread. The scent of olive oil, salt, and herbs wafted over the preparation area.

"How'd you know I would need bread?"

"I didn't." He set the flat Italian bread on a cutting board. "I, too, pursued what I felt led to make. Now you have revealed why!"

Mia's heart danced. She loved creating with this group. The pressure wasn't on her to do more. There was shared energy and excitement as she joined those equally passionate about the art of cooking.

The kitchen took on a rhythm as each cook pursued a specific role. Chef Gino whistled as he tossed the avocado in the air and caught it. "I will slice and spice this while you prepare the meat, Mia."

She set an iron skillet on the stove and turned the burner on medium heat, then found a cutting board and butcher's knife. Mia sliced the marbled meat into thin pieces, sprinkling salt and pepper over them.

Bandana's hands were a blur as she chopped up the jalapeño. The tattooed chef washed the arugula and tomato, then moved back to the cooling bread. He cut two pieces and set them on a plate.

Chef Gino raised a spatula. "Question for the new chef!"

Mia looked up from her spot in front of the gas stove. "Yes?"

"What happens if others do not like your creation?"

"I try a new recipe?"

"Do not change for the critic! We are responsible to create with the Creator and then serve it to the hungry. If others don't like it, that doesn't invalidate the dish. We cook to satisfy body and soul rather than on order. If someone prefers another dish, let them learn to cook that rather than simply critique what another has been called to do."

Mia felt as if chains had fallen from her heart. She grated the Gruyère cheese and sprinkled it on top of the almost done pieces of tenderloin.

"Now, let us see how Chef Mia's desire will come together."

She scooped the meat and melted cheese up with a spatula and slid it onto the open-faced bread. Celtic Chef added fresh tomato and arugula. From the side, Chef Gino delicately placed avocado wedges on top of those items. Bandana drizzled jalapeño honey sauce over the avocado and then topped it with the other piece of focaccia bread. Working in unison, each focused on their part of the creation. It was like a dance that grew in intensity as it progressed.

A scowl crossed Chef Gino's face. Mia followed his gaze to a man across from them with scars on his face and arms. He wore brown slacks and a navy-blue T-shirt.

"Was anyone expecting company?" Chef Gino asked. The other chefs shook their heads. He took off his hat and strutted across the kitchen until he was face to chest with the tall dreadlocked stranger. "May I help you?"

The towering figure's scars were even more pronounced as he stepped into the light. He stared intently at Mia. "She will come with me."

Celtic Chef stepped in front of Mia as Bandana tightened her grip on the knife. The huge arms of the stranger brushed against the hanging pots and pans as he approached them.

"You will leave my kitchen now!" Chef Gino shouted.

The man looked past the chefs, directly into Mia's eyes. "Did Iona tell you about me?"

Lost in the joy of cooking, Mia had momentarily forgotten the larger mission. "Iona said I had an enemy here."

"She's right about that."

Mia panicked. The muscular man could easily overpower the chefs or outrun her if she tried to flee. Chef Celtic stood between them but looked more uncertain by the second.

The stranger shoved Chef Celtic out of his way. Mia felt like she was about to hyperventilate.

"Hey!" Bandana waved her knife toward the stranger. "Unless you want some new scars, leave now."

A golden glow became visible within the man's scars. He raised his right hand toward Bandana and rays of light shot from his fingers, knocking the knife out of her hand. Chef Gino charged the intruder.

Mia had to get out of here. Her hand went to the jacket pocket. She took out the pouch and scanned the words on the vials. She'd only have one shot at this.

Her passion was awakened by these bohemians. She grabbed the vial with the word *Awaken*. But what did it require? She didn't have time to try every ingredient in the kitchen. She looked at the red container with an engraved heart. The shape and color reminded her of a perfume bottle. Was that a clue? What if the scents of the kitchen were what it required? Could she bottle the atmosphere around her?

The man with scars shoved Chef Gino aside while keeping his eyes on Mia. She took the cork off the vial and held it high. "No, stop!" the dreadlocked intruder screamed and ran at her. She sealed it as he grabbed her arm. Mia fell against a metal prep station but couldn't escape his hold.

He lifted her to a standing position. "We're done here. You're coming with me."

the shift
to with

TAKE HEART

Her entire life, Mia has felt like she didn't quite fit in. No one shared her interests or understood her dreams. But then she discovers a place where kindred spirits passionately pursue the very things that make her come alive.

Now her heart is being awakened. Which is exactly what she needs at this stage of her journey. We can't be fully present to God or others if our hearts have flat-lined. That's why Scripture (Proverbs 4:23) tells us nothing is more important than protecting our hearts. How is your heart doing at this moment? Are you aware of the things you do each day that either numb or nurture your heart? If you can't name specific ways you are taking care of your heart, then it is probably in need of attention.

> If you can't name specific ways you are taking care of your heart, then it is probably in need of attention.

What if our deepest desires, the very things that make our hearts come alive, actually serve as a source code that draws us to God? I believe God instills a unique set of interests and talent within each of us, knowing the more we pursue them, the more we encounter Him. God creates a world of wonder and then places a corresponding wonder in each of us. Imagine it. The very things in life that we're drawn to were made for us.

His motive in giving you specific talents isn't primarily so you'll be productive. *Here's your gift. Now get busy making things happen.* It is so your desires can find their fulfillment in Him. Productivity and efficiency aren't what He's most interested in. They measure the external performance but never the internal rhythm of your heart. God doesn't need your help as much as He wants your heart. Whenever you start to focus more on your talents and gifts than on Him, you miss the main invitation. Which is to pursue them together. With Him.

God's offer is primarily relational and internal. How to *be* more rather than simply *do* more.

Imagine stepping into your job, home, or classroom today alert to His presence. Watching what He is up to. Following His lead. Leaning into Him for what seems impossible. Your heart will come alive. Not just because of what you are doing but because of who you are doing it with.

> God's offer is primarily relational and internal. How to *be* more rather than simply *do* more.

You were never meant to pursue the things you love as a solo endeavor. Why would we try to create in isolation when God never did? The Creation account in Genesis makes it clear that all three members of the Trinity were intimately involved in the act of creation. Our gifts and talents increase in vision and impact when we pursue them in creative fellowship rather than in isolation.

The bohemian chefs refuse to reduce their art to formulaic rules. They know an awakened heart is the first ingredient to any creative undertaking. And it is in their kitchen that Mia receives her first taste of this new way to live.

sinking

Mia clutched the blood-red vial in her hand as the stranger hovered over her.

"Get up, now."

"What do you want from me?" As she spoke, the vial began to vibrate. Mia felt the atmosphere around her reverberate as well. The dreadlocked intruder kept an iron-tight grip on her arm, but she was starting to fade away. She blinked and was in the elevator, alone. Then she was back in the kitchen, trapped by the stranger.

He placed both hands on her shoulders. "Do not disappear on me." But Mia wasn't in control of what was happening. The kitchen seemed to melt around her and the scarred man's voice grew more distant. She felt like she was falling away from him, though there was no up or down. Merely away.

When things swam back into focus, she was in the elevator. This time, she remained there. The vial saved her from the intruder, but also ripped Mia from one of the happiest experiences of her life.

It seemed every time something good happened, it was snatched away from her. She missed the chefs and hoped they were safe.

Mia carefully placed the *Awaken* vial back in the leather pouch. She put it in her jacket pocket and pushed the 3 button. Mia jerked her hand back. The panel was hot to the touch. The elevator felt like a sauna.

The automated voice announced, "Level 2 complete. Going up." Beads of sweat trickled down her forehead. As the elevator slowed, Mia tossed her jacket to the floor. She moved back a few feet, unsure what was on the other side.

The door opened to a desert. Swirling sand blew inside the elevator, making it impossible to see more than a few feet in front of her. Mia squinted to keep the grit out of her eyes. She fled the metal box but stumbled and fell in the shifting sand. From her hands and knees, she took in her surroundings.

Not good.

There were no buildings or people . . . just endless desert and blazing sun.

No way I'm getting stuck in this hellhole. Mia wiped the sweaty grit from her eyes and mouth, then pivoted to see the still-open elevator door. She rushed into the elevator and pushed the number 4 button. The door closed, shutting out the sandstorm. She fell back against the far wall and slid down. There was a foot of sand on the floor. Mia spit the grit from her mouth.

The elevator wasn't moving. Mia pulled herself up and hit the button for the next floor again. Nothing. Then a familiar voice came through the speaker.

"Mia, stop running from your Story."

"Iona?" Mia looked around her. "Where are you?"

"As close as I can get for the moment."

"Some madman tried to capture me at the last level."

"It sounds like you've met the enemy."

"I got away. But then the elevator opened to a desert. I came here to find my dad. Not go through some survival course on steroids."

"You can do this, Mia. The only way to get what you desire is to stay on the journey."

"Fine, but I'm doing this my way."

"Your way? That's not how it works."

"I'm not wasting my time in that desert."

"Why do you desire efficiency more than transformation? Your father —"

Static came through the speaker. The elevator lights flickered. Then it was silent.

"My father what? Answer me, Iona!"

Mia swept her hair from her eyes. "I'm skipping this level," she shouted at the speaker. "That's my choice." She pushed the fourth-floor button. As the elevator rose, the temperature immediately cooled.

Anything will be better than —

She was thrown into the far wall as the elevator jerked to a stop. She fell to the floor. Dazed, she grabbed the waist-high rail and pulled herself up. She rubbed her forehead. *Maybe skipping a floor isn't such a good idea.*

The sound of clanging gears and smell of burning rubber flooded the small space. The elevator shook violently, as if a giant was yanking the main cable back and forth.

With a loud screech, the left corner of the floor ripped from the wall. The hole was big enough to fall through. Mia screamed as she grabbed hold of the rail inches from the opening.

What have I done?

She peered into the hole and imagined falling through it. She wondered if she would see glimpses of each level — the kitchen, the ocean, and the coffee shop — on her way down.

Mia used the rail on the back wall to inch her way to the controls. Trying to bypass a floor would destroy the elevator . . . and her. Mia stretched toward the panel and jabbed the number 3 button. She preferred the desert to this death box.

"Level 3 incomplete."

"That's why I'm trying to go back, you stupid —" But the elevator didn't move.

She paced back and forth, stepping over her jacket. Her stomach tightened. The pouch. It was still in her jacket pocket. She ran into the desert earlier without the vials. Maybe that's why the elevator had remained. If filling the vials with the right substance caused the elevator to go up, maybe empty ones had the opposite effect.

She took the pouch from her jacket and pulled the two empty vials—*Identity* and *Together*—from the thin strap that held them in place. She wasn't sure which one she'd need for this level.

The elevator awoke with a tremor. She lost her balance on the uneven floor, hitting her shoulder hard on a side wall. As the elevator began to go down, the heat grew unbearable. She held the rail for balance as she placed the pouch in her jacket pocket. She grabbed one arm of her jacket and tied it around the rail. She couldn't risk leaving her jacket on the floor, where it—and the two filled vials—could fall through the hole.

The elevator slowed. She was back at Level 3. The door slid a third of the way open, then stuck. Grains of sand flew through the space, pelting Mia's skin and eyes. She had to protect the two vials. As she went to put them in her jeans pocket, the elevator plunged a half foot, then caught. She stumbled back and a vial fell from her hand. She tried to find it but couldn't see anything with the blowing sandstorm. She thrust the remaining vial in her pocket and used both hands to feel her way forward. Gripping the bent metal door, she pushed with all her strength. It only moved another few inches but that was enough. She had to get out before she choked on sand or the elevator fell apart.

Standing in the desert, she coughed and wiped the grit from her eyes. The sand still blew, but in the wide open space it didn't feel like an assault. She stared at the desert. Just sand, sky, and dunes. She glanced back. The elevator had disappeared this time. Hopefully that was a sign she had the right vial. Either way, she was committed. The only way up was to complete this level. She shielded her eyes from the sun's relentless glare, missing her sunglasses. There were no landmarks to guide her, so she decided to head away from the sun. At least that way she could see without squinting.

"Mia, stop!" She turned to see the man with scars approaching.

Adrenaline shot through her veins. "Get away from me!" There was a large dune, less than a hundred feet in front of her. She ran to it.

He followed, but appeared to be in no hurry.

Mia rounded the dune from the left and stopped abruptly. On the other side was a man in a teak chair, a book in one hand and a bag of sunflower seeds in the other. Maybe it was his glasses, but he reminded Mia of a college professor reviewing his textbook before class.

"Please. Help." She could hardly speak from sprinting in the sand.

The man in khakis and a blue button-down shirt set the items down by his chair and rose. "I'm Asher. What's going on?"

"A man is chasing me."

A sense of calm strength radiated from him. "Let me handle this." Mia stood several feet behind him. He didn't appear to be strong enough to stop the man with scars. She wanted as much of a head start as possible should he fail.

The man with scars rounded the dune. He seemed surprised to see the two of them together. Asher pointed a finger at him. "You have no claim on this woman. Leave her alone."

The man with dreadlocks stood his ground, a mix of sarcasm and disbelief on his face. "You act as if this is your desert."

"Don't cross me." Asher glared. "I play for keeps."

Flashes of gold light began to glow from within the scarred man's wounds. Asher took a few steps back. Mia thought the bespectacled man was about to retreat. Instead, he slowly lifted his hands to the sky. As he did, sand began to rise from the desert floor and swirl around the man in dreadlocks. In seconds, he was trapped within a cocoon of moving sand.

Asher turned to her. "Now where were we?"

Mia pointed to the captive prisoner. Light pulsated from within the sand cocoon.

Asher put his arm in front of Mia. "Back up. It's not going to hold."

The sand exploded and the scarred figure took a step forward. "You're going to have to do better than that."

"Am I?"

The towering man suddenly doubled over in pain, falling to his knees.

"What's happening, Asher?"

"The sand that surrounded him earlier has seeped into his scars. It is having a rather toxic effect on him." The intruder was now writhing on the desert floor.

Asher adjusted his glasses. "You should have listened, Ryder."

Mia's eyes widened. "You know him?"

"We've had many . . . encounters. Your instinct to flee was good."

She wiped sweat from her brow and turned to Asher. "I'm Mia, by the way. And this isn't the first time I've seen Ryder. He chased me on another level."

Asher raised his eyebrow. "Level?"

"Just get me out of this place."

"Follow me," Asher said.

They stepped to the side of the intruder and began their trek through the sand. It was hard for her to judge their progress since there were no landmarks. Yet every step away from Ryder calmed her nerves a bit more.

The sun beat down on them. Mia was moments from a heatstroke yet Asher didn't seem to break a sweat. "You must be used to this weather. Thanks for coming to my rescue. He is relentless."

"Happy to help. But even that won't hold him long. We must keep moving."

"So how did you do the whole sand trick back there?"

"I can teach you many ways to stop Ryder, if you like."

"This is all so different than the real world."

Asher stopped walking and looked at her. "Where do you think you are, Mia?"

"In a story." She looked at the desert before her. "A really wild story."

Asher looked concerned. "Did a woman named Iona send you here?" he asked as he led her forward.

Her heart beat faster. "You know Iona?"

"Quite well, I'm afraid. She loves throwing people into stories. It's a game for her. If you don't mind me asking, how did she convince you to play it?"

"I'm here to find my father."

"And you think he's in this desert?"

"I don't know where he is. But Iona said she sent him on a similar path more than twenty years ago."

"Mia, I know we just met. But your father isn't here. You are on your own. You need to accept that reality rather than get lost in Iona's story for the wrong reason."

"She told me this journey will help me find the Blue Door . . . and possibly him."

Asher tapped his temple and gave a knowing grin. "A blue door? Doesn't that sound a bit over the top?"

Mia stared at the ground, trying not to lose hope.

"I don't mean to sound harsh. I know this is important to you. What will happen if you reach this supposed door?"

"She didn't exactly say."

He nodded and pulled a small package of sunflower seeds from his khakis. "Let's start with what you do know."

"Okay. We arrived at this old building where Iona told me that I had to take the elevator to each floor."

"Iona was here?" He poured some seeds into his hand.

"Barely. She knew there was an enemy so she didn't stay long."

"But she had no qualms leaving you to contend with Ryder."

"She warned me about him. And said I'd have a helper as well. Thank you for being that, Asher."

He tilted his head forward and smiled. "Would you like some sunflower seeds?"

"I think that would just make me more thirsty."

"Then please continue."

She increased her gate to keep up with his brisk pace. "Strange things happen every time the elevator door opens. But she gave me four glass vials to help me move forward. If my dad's alive, I'm going to find him."

"Mia, you have great intentions." He took in a deep breath and exhaled. "But I know this desert and, trust me, your dad isn't here. Neither is some mystical door." He stopped walking and placed his hand on her shoulder. "I also know Iona. She seems kind, but why would the person warning you about such a dangerous place drop you right in the middle of it?"

"Why would she want to hurt me?"

He shrugged. "This is the woman who sent your father on a wild goose chase. And he's been gone how long?" He looked into her eyes. "I can help undo what Iona's gotten you into. But only if that's what you want."

"I want out of this desert."

"That's why I'm here. To help redirect the ones Iona misdirects. To help you appreciate what you already have back home."

"So how do I leave?"

"To get out of this story, you just need to embrace reality rather than run from it. The glass vials symbolize this misguided trip. Call off this search for your father and some blue door. You'll never be content with the life you had until you quit chasing after some make-believe fantasy. Dreams aren't helpful if they distract you from reality."

That resonated with Mia. Maybe the way to move forward was to end this search for what didn't exist anyway. Truth is, she was no more likely to find her dad than she was the blue door or the man on the moon.

Asher smiled. "Your future is yours alone. Just give me the vials." He held out his hand. "Doing so takes their power away and shows you are done with this wild goose chase."

"I only have one vial. The others are in the elevator."

"That's fine, Mia. It's just symbolic. Your words have power. Give me the vial and say, 'I quit.' Then I'll get you home."

She recalled Iona's warning: *If you quit, you won't make it out of the Story.* But could she trust

Iona? It was because of her that Mia was stuck in this desert.

She reached into her pocket for the vial. Then an image flashed in her mind. She was in the truck with her dad. They were laughing. They were together.

She could give up on Iona and the hunt for some blue door . . . but not her father.

Her eyes met Asher's. "I can't quit. I have no idea what I'm doing or how to overcome this desert, but I've got to keep searching for my dad."

He nodded. "There is another way. But it is only for those strong enough to handle it."

"I am, Asher. Tell me how."

"Through sheer willpower. It is you against the desert. It won't be easy. And I can't help you. You must do this on your own."

"I'll do it."

"Good, Mia. Repeat after me, 'I can overcome this desert in my own strength.'"

"I can overcome this desert in my own strength."

The sand beneath her feet began to shift.

"What's happening?"

"It's working. Remember what I said earlier. Your words have power. Now say, 'I can do whatever I set my mind to. I will not let this desert hold me back.'"

She did and her feet slid into the sticky, soupy grains.

"Is this quicksand?" Oozing sand covered her ankles.

"Yes, the desert is fighting back."

"What do I do?" Mia felt herself begin to panic.

"Try harder, Mia. It's all up to you."

"I can do this. I won't be stopped." Mia used every ounce of strength to pull herself out, but the more she fought, the deeper she sunk. Knee-deep in the mush, she felt as if she were in the middle of a giant hourglass, slowly sinking through the hole.

Glass? It was her only hope. She reached into her back pocket and pulled out the vial. She raised her right hand above her head, determined not to let the blue container get stuck in the sand approaching her waist.

The only thing around her was sand. What else could the vial require? She scooped some sand into it and waited. Nothing happened.

"Asher, it's not working. Help me!"

"I can't, Mia. I told you it was all up to you." He spit a sunflower seed into the sand.

"And you're failing."

"The vial just needs the right ingredient."

He stood there, expressionless.

"Asher, please. I don't want to die." Her right arm was raised above the sand, the vial in her fingers. "Take it!"

He lifted the small blue bottle from her hand and looked at it, like a relic he'd long sought.

"See if you can find other—"

He let the vial drop and crunched it under his heel. Fragments of blue glass lay in the sand.

"That was my only way out! Are you crazy?"

Asher's lips curled into a menacing grin. "Actually, yes. I'm the one Iona warned you about. And I love to break things."

The quicksand crept up to her shoulders.

"I broke your father's spirit years ago. Iona never should have encouraged such a weak man to take this journey. Now she's made the same mistake with his daughter."

"I'll find a way out." Mia squirmed and flexed to loosen the sand's hold on her.

Asher smirked. "Brave words for a woman sinking by the second. But yes, by all means, keep trying in your own strength."

"If you hadn't destroyed the vial—"

"Do you want a piece of your lifesaving vial?" He bent and picked up a fragment from the sand. Mia opened her hand for it. Leaning in, he pressed it against her palm. Then flicked his wrist. She screamed as the glass cut her skin, blood trickling from her palm down the length of her upraised arm. "Was that helpful?" He tossed the bloodied shard to the ground.

Then Asher walked away from Mia, leaving her to die the same way she'd lived . . . alone.

"I hate you," she yelled, the sand compressing her chest making it hard to breath.

He stopped and glanced back at her. "If it's any consolation, you lasted longer than your father." Asher turned, humming softly as he walked toward the horizon.

the shift
to with

DON'T QUIT

It begins with a few grains of doubt. Yet the sand quickly multiplies the more we give in to our anxieties and try to solve life's problems in our own strength. And the enemy does everything in his power to initiate and amplify the very things that got us trapped in the first place.

If we don't address the issues that gave birth to the fears, resentment, greed, lust, shame, envy, and, well, the list is long—then one day we look up and find that what was once a sandbox is now the Sahara desert.

Everyone's desert is custom-made. Mine would have little effect on you. But man, that dry place has taken me out more times than I care to admit. Your desert is made up of the things that derail or defeat you.

Whatever gives birth to our deserts, the end result is that we find ourselves parched and

> ## Your desert is made up of the things that derail or defeat you.

weary in the burning sand. We try to escape by running from it, but that never breaks its hold on us. The more we run, the farther we find ourselves from our original dreams and stories. I'm guessing you already know that's true.

Then we try to overcome it in our own strength. But our overreliance on self is what got us into the desert in the first place. That's the problem—not the antidote for breaking free. Alone, we are no match for the enemy or the desert. Without God, we remain residents of the Orphan Realm.

What is the dry and dusty place you find yourself stuck in? Think of where you go when you feel lost, parched, and isolated. There's the Desert of Regret. Or perhaps the Desert of Striving, which begins with the subtle agreement that life is up to you. Maybe it's the Desert of the Overwhelmed, where there never seems to be enough time and you live from a place of scarcity. There are as many deserts as there are people. Some of us have multiple deserts.

The first step is to know and to name your desert. The next step is to realize you can't set yourself free. It is in this stripped away place that our identity either disintegrates or is forged anew.

Yes, it's hard to recognize the possibility for rescue when the enemy has you in quicksand and you're sinking fast. But it's hard to experience a miracle until you reach the end of yourself and are completely dependent on a savior. Which is exactly where Mia finds herself.

> It is in this stripped away place that our identity either disintegrates or is forged anew.

kintsugi

The sand slid over Mia's shoulders and gathered around her neck. So this is how her story would end . . . in a Story. More than the loss of her own life, she grieved the realization that she'd never see her father again.

The cut on her palm stung, but that was the least of her worries. In minutes, she wouldn't be able to breathe. To keep the sticky substance from her mouth, she titled her chin up. All she could see was blurry sky as a mix of sweat and sand stung her eyes. She kept her hands above her. The sand moved from her chin to her lips. She closed her mouth, taking breaths through her nose.

Someone approached, but Mia couldn't lower her head to see who it was. With the quicksand over her mouth, there was no way to speak.

As the sand rose over her nose, she squeezed her eyes shut. From the dark, Mia felt strong hands grip her wrists. One moment she was slipping farther under, in the next, she was rising out of the sand. The quicksand fought to keep its hold, but it was no match for the strength of her rescuer.

Mia gasped, air filling her lungs as her body was lifted out and set gently on solid ground. She was covered in gritty mush. Exhausted both physically and emotionally, it took every bit of energy to raise her head to see her rescuer.

It was Ryder. He looked like a cross between a medieval knight and a modern day cowboy in dreadlocks. Deep scars ran across his face and muscular forearms. He gently wiped the sand from her eyes and mouth with a cloth. Then held a canteen of water to her dry lips and poured cool liquid down her parched throat.

Water never tasted so good. After draining the canteen, she slowly sat. "Why did you save me?"

"That's why I'm here. To watch over you."

"I thought you wanted to kill me."

"You mistake intensity for ill intent."

"But all you've done is chase me."

"That's because all you've done is run from me."

"*You're* the help Iona promised?"

Ryder sat next to her and pulled his knees into his chest. "Yes. I am a Watchman. My goal is to watch over you and help you make it through this Story. And I almost lost you to Asher. He wanted the desert to devour you. He'll do whatever it takes to break you."

"Thanks for pulling me from the quicksand. But Asher destroyed my only way out." She pointed to the blue shards glistening in the sun. "I'm stuck here."

Ryder walked to the broken glass. He picked up each piece, placing them carefully into his large palm. He tossed the cork to her.

Mia saw red on one shard. She glanced at her palm. The blood around her wound and on her arm had dried. It reminded her of when Iona purposely cut her own finger in the coffee shop. "When I entered this Story, Iona warned me of the stakes. She said, 'Get cut, you bleed. Get killed, you die.'"

"That's true. You can get hurt here. But you can also get healed here."

He traced the etching on the blood stained fragment with his finger. "It says *Identity*."

"Thanks to Asher, that vial's a total loss."

He returned and sat next to her. "You worry about the loss of a vial more than the loss of your identity?"

"I worry about being stuck here and never finding my father. My identity doesn't matter much at this point. The first two vials had the words *Expectant* and *Awaken*. But why be expectant or awaken my heart just to discover how broken it is?"

"Your heart's been broken a long time, Mia. What's being offered is a chance to heal it. But for that to happen, you must first be awakened and expectant."

Mia wiped sweat from her eyes and looked at the jagged cuts etched in his skin. She was embarrassed at her earlier fear of Ryder.

He took a handful of sand and let it sift through his fingers.

Mia sighed. "I hate sand. Even the vial didn't want any."

He swept his dreadlocks behind his

shoulders. "Sand represents the desert. Not the way out."

"Why did the sand cause you so much pain earlier?"

"Asher attacked me in the place of my greatest strength. He tried to bury the power of my light with lies from the desert. Filling my scars with sand. But I resisted...and he ran away."

"Earlier, you said this wasn't Asher's desert. Is that true?"

"Yes. That's why his traps couldn't hold me and why he was so quick to leave. He doesn't have ultimate control over this place."

"Why not?"

"Because it is your desert. It represents your inner life, Mia."

"So this is my fault?"

"It's your creation, not your fault. Since you were born, Asher's goal has been to expand your desert grain by grain through the pain he's brought to your life. Those wounds caused you to believe life is all up to you."

She shook her head. "So when Asher said it was up to me to defeat the desert —"

"He was provoking you. He knew the more

you tried to control the desert from your own strength, the more power you'd give it. His plan almost worked. The desert was literally devouring you."

"He said my words have power."

"They do. For good or for harm."

"Why did Iona include such a dangerous place for my journey?"

"Because the desert is part of every person's story. It doesn't look quite like this in the real world. The enemy prefers to remain hidden, so you assume what comes against you is just part of life. Or worse, your own fault."

Ryder set the five pieces of glass on the sand before him, like a puzzle waiting to be assembled. He held two blue fragments, turning them until the edges fit.

"It's impossible, Ryder. That vial is a lost cause."

"The world has always been quick to discard what's broken. Ancient Japanese artisans discovered a way to make the broken beautiful again through the art of kintsugi."

"Kin what?"

He smiled. "It is the art of repairing what has been shattered by infusing golden lacquer in the fractured places."

"But that just highlights the brokenness."

"That is the point. Rather than hide the imperfections, they highlight them by filling the cracks with liquid gold. They view the repaired item as even more valuable, because it is now unique from all other vessels." As he spoke, he smeared a golden substance on the jagged sides of the two shards. He then pressed them tight while the liquid hardened.

"How are you doing that?"

"When the Creator heals you, then you are infused with His healing power."

Mia looked down at the sand, unsure how to ask Ryder her question. "But if you've been healed, why are you covered in scars?"

"Remember kintsugi, Mia. The goal isn't to hide the broken places but to redeem them. My scars are like my story, tattooed on my body."

"I've always kept my scars hidden. Why spotlight the places of hurt and betrayal?"

"What's highlighted is the redemption. It's counterintuitive, but when the Creator redeems us where the enemy tried to break us, our scars then become areas of strength. Neither the desert nor your scars can tell you who you are. The enemy often attacks us at our points of purpose. That's why the areas of your life that have been most opposed offer clues to your unique calling."

Ryder took another piece and aligned it with the two fused ones. The original shape of the vial was beginning to take form. He applied gold lacquer to the seams. "Think back to when you were a young girl, Mia. What stirred your imagination? What were the areas of interest you fell into and never wanted to fall out of?"

Mia made lines in the sand with her finger. "I loved when our neighbors and relatives would gather for a meal. I would help my dad plan the menu, prepare the food, and set the table. We made feasts that brought people together. After my dad vanished, the community meals ended. As a teen, I worked in restaurants. The hours were brutal but I thought being around people and food might remind me of those happier times. But they just wanted me to prepare the food faster. So I learned to put my head down and get things done."

She sat for a moment, reliving the scene in her mind before continuing. "One day, my boss handed me a sealed envelope, told me not to open it but to give it to my mother. I did with trembling hands. I thought I'd been fired. To my surprise, he praised my hard work. Said my productivity would take me places if I'd just lose my fascination with cooking and realize it was simply my way to earn a paycheck."

"What did your mother think?" Ryder asked as he took the fourth piece of glass and aligned it with the others.

"I'd been invisible to her since my father left, an irritant that reminded her of him. But that note made her smile. She saw I could get things done. And I saw the harder I worked, the more she noticed me. From then on, I embraced productivity and performance as the way to her affection. I thought maybe if I did more, she would love me more."

Ryder nodded. "Scars like that run deep."

"It's in the past. I'm over it."

He raised an eyebrow. "Are you?"

"It's like the nightmare I had last night. Ravens flew into my home and covered me. Their beaks and claws dug into my flesh until I passed out. But then I woke up and shook it off. Nightmares can't leave scars."

"Visible or not, all scars leave their mark.

And Mia, you don't get through this life without being wounded. Most of the time, the scars stay buried deep inside us."

She felt a wave of hopelessness. "I thought I could find my dad by stepping into this story. But it's too much. My whole life has been about loss. I lose what matters most. And it's happening again here."

Ryder set the partially repaired vial down. "Mia—"

"It's true. I lost my father when I was a girl. I lost my job today. Then I lost the chance to join a larger food company." She gave a half-hearted laugh. "I'm here because I lost my way home."

"You have suffered great loss, but you didn't lose those things. They have been stolen from you."

"Either way, I'll never get them back."

"Maybe not in the way you would guess. But the Creator specializes in making all things new. He can restore both the past and the future. You just have to remember who you are first."

She shrugged. "A chef?"

"That's what you love doing. Go deeper. Otherwise, what happens when you get too old to cook one day? Who will you be then?"

Mia sat in the sand, speechless.

Ryder picked up a large shard of glass, covered the rough edge in golden lacquer, and set it in a perfectly matching gap.

"Look at me, Mia. Who am I?"

"You said you're a Watchman."

"That's what I do. Who I am goes deeper than what I do." His face beamed. "I am a son of the Creator. So I ask again, who are you?"

She paused. "A daughter of the Creator?"

"Yes, Mia, yes!" A huge smile covered his face. "That is your core identity—one that can't be earned or stolen. It is the foundation for everything else in your life." He placed the final fragment into place. The golden substance now ran throughout the blue glass, holding the previously shattered pieces together. Ryder blew on the vial to help the liquid harden.

She looked at the repaired vial. "It's almost as good as new."

His eyes twinkled. "It's better than new."

Mia no longer saw her scars in the same way. They reflected attacks on her identity from the world and from the enemy. And in some cases, her own poor choices. "How do I redeem my scars, Ryder?"

"The Creator can put the fragments of your life and heart back together with His healing light. Simply give the pieces to Him."

She nodded and walked several feet into the desert. Then kneeled and spoke words between her and the Creator. After a while, she stepped back to Ryder. Tears streamed down her cheeks.

"Ryder, if my false beliefs made this desert, then can I unmake it?"

"You can't overcome it alone. But with Him, you can."

She paced as her focus shifted from the sinking sand to the rising hope within her. "I spent my life trying to control things because I assumed I was on my own. That lie created this desert. I thought I could overcome it in my own strength, which almost killed me. When that didn't work, I pleaded with the enemy to rescue me. But I never thought to cry out to my Creator. I will not make that mistake again."

"You're learning, Mia. Remember who you are and whose you are. Speak your identity and let His healing light shine from you."

"I am a child of the Creator. And as His daughter, I can't be an orphan because I am never alone." As she spoke, a low golden glow began to emanate from the cut on her palm. She held out her shaking hand. "Ryder, what is happening to me?"

"Kintsugi isn't just for broken vessels, Mia."

The light grew more intense, then spread from her palm to her arm. "What—"

"The kintsugi is strengthening all the broken places within you, the seen and unseen places."

Her radiance grew stronger. She raised her arms. "My identity cannot be taken from me or defined for me. Not by the world and not by the enemy."

"That's it, Mia. As you speak truth, the desert loses its hold over you."

She looked at him. "But the vial. As long as it's empty, I remain here."

"Iona sent you here to discover your identity. Bottle that instead of the desert."

Mia's eyes widened. "Kintsugi . . . that's what the vial needs!"

"Yes, but it's what you needed first." He rose and handed her the vial.

She was mesmerized at the glistening gold that held the blue vial together. "You're right. This is better than before." Light pulsed up and down her arms, visible under her skin.

Ryder looked at the brilliant sky and then at Mia. "It's time."

She held the open vial against her palm. Golden rays flowed into the container from the place where Asher had cut her. She quickly sealed it with the cork. Healing beams surged within, like lightning in a bottle. The radiant light contained rather than captured.

She felt the familiar twinge in the atmosphere. The vial was satisfied.

"I'm sorry I ran from you. Thank you for reminding me who I am."

"I will watch over you, Mia."

She closed her eyes and felt a massive release. The desert had lost its hold of her.

the shift
to with

THE SCARS OF YOUR STORY

We all have scars. Most unseen. Betrayal from those we trusted. Silence when we needed support. Conditional love based on our performance. Hearts shattered. Though the wounds are invisible, they cut deep.

The world teaches us to hide our scars. They feel like a sign of weakness, a source of shame, or represent a past we'd rather forget.

Yet to fully break free from your desert, you must go into the scars of your stories. Without question, this is one of the most challenging parts of the journey. It's why so many avoid their Stories. Scars scare us. Yet trying to hide or forget the painful parts of our story takes away an

> You must go into the scars of your stories. Without question, this is one of the most challenging parts of the journey.

essential aspect of our identity. As Mia discovered, skipping this level isn't the way out.

Though difficult, this process is actually an act of kindness when done with God. It will be a tremendous balm for your soul as He reinterprets your scars in a way that brings healing and redemption to those wounds. The scars that brought shame or harm weren't from God nor were they meant for good. But what if the scars, once redeemed, can help lead you out of the desert into your truer identity?

The opposition you feel around your life is specific and personal. The enemy of your story is actually a created being gone bad. Ancient Scripture reveals that God created not just the heavens and the earth, but also the angels. Lucifer appears to have been one of God's most creative angels. But don't miss this point, he is a created being. The enemy isn't just the opposite of God, he is so much less. Only God is the uncreated Creator.

Jealous that God was worshipped rather than him, he convinced a third of the angels to turn against the Creator. Imagine how God's heart must have felt. What if a third of all that you've created turned against you? What you once breathed life into was suddenly obsessed with your destruction.

A war in heaven followed where God defeated the rebellion led by Lucifer. Our enemy is a fallen creation who hates those who embrace their identity and create with God. He chose the wrong story and tries to make us do the same.

When we breathe life into this world, we remind our enemy of the Creator. When we create with the Creator, he cringes at his lost fellowship with God. The enemy can't create from nothing. He can only distort and try to destroy God's creations.

> Our enemy is a fallen creation who hates those who embrace their identity and create with God. He chose the wrong story and tries to make us do the same.

He knows as long as we live and create in isolation, the life is stolen from our calling. When we believe his lies rather than stay with God, the only thing we are creating is a larger desert.

The good news is, our words really do have power. When we submit to God and resist the enemy, he must flee (James 4:7). The key is to start with God. It is through and with Him that you will defeat the desert and derail the enemy's attacks.

The Creator can't wait to redeem the scars of your story. Do you feel that breeze? The desert is losing its hold of you . . . and your scars are starting to glow with His healing light of kintsugi.

diner

Elevator music wove in and out of Mia's consciousness. She awoke in musty darkness. Lifting her head, she realized she was facedown on the elevator carpet. She groaned as she pushed herself up. A pulsating light was flickering. She looked at her arms but they were no longer glowing.

It was the vial. What appeared to be gold electricity shimmered within the blue bottle.

The elevator had definitely seen better days. The small space reeked of sweat, overheated gears, and wet sand. A gaping hole was in the left back corner where the floor was pulled from the wall. And the metal door, though closed, was bent so badly she wasn't sure it would ever open again.

Mia stood and stretched. Her jacket was still tied to the rail. The *Together* vial, the one she had dropped before entering the desert, was still on the floor. She picked it up, glad it hadn't rolled into the hole. She undid the loose knot in the arm of her jacket and took it from the rail. She put her jacket on and placed the kintsugi container and the remaining empty vial back in the leather holder.

She hated the desert, but a new strength pulsed through her. Ryder was right. Knowing your identity changes everything. She pushed the button for the next level.

"Level 3 complete. Going up." The elevator jerked to life, straining to make it to the floor above. She had no idea what awaited her but felt a new confidence. It could be anything from the dark side of the moon to a yellow brick road and it wouldn't surprise her. Or take her out.

The elevator dinged and made a rough stop. The dented door slid partially open and a cool breeze greeted her. Mia squeezed through the opening to an expansive wheat field.

As she walked through the grain, she held her palms out. They brushed the tips of the wheat stalks to the left and right. This wasn't just any wheat field. It was the farm she grew up on.

Mia looked down. She was wearing her favorite sneakers from when she was a teenager. Her jeans were different too. And her jacket had morphed into her favorite turquoise sweater from high school. She ran her tongue over her teeth. Braces. *Why am I in my sixteen-year-old clothes . . . and body?*

Her hand went to the sweater pocket. The only thing in it was only a folded piece of paper. She pulled it out and opened it. Seeing the handwriting, she knew immediately who it was from. And what it said. She had lived this scene before. The note was from Brandon, telling her he'd decided not to take her to the homecoming dance after all. Feeling totally unwanted, she'd come to the wheat fields behind her home to be alone and grieve.

Mia knew how this evening would play out. As others prepared for the dance, she would go into the house and cry herself to sleep. Of all the places for the story to take her, this was the last memory she wanted to relive.

I'd almost choose the desert over this. Let's make this quick.

But how? The pouch of vials was missing. This time she hadn't left her jacket or the vials in the elevator. Her jacket had transformed into a sweater while she was wearing it. If the vials went wherever her jacket did, she was stuck here. She had no desire to permanently be sixteen again. She frantically patted her back jean pockets. Nothing. Her hands raced to the front ones. She let out a sigh of relief. The remaining vial was in her right front jeans pocket. She'd worry about the other vials later. At least she had the one that needed to be filled.

"Hey, girl."

She turned to see her father approaching. Her eyes grew wide. "Dad?"

This couldn't be. He'd left so long ago. Yet here he was, back home, wearing his favorite pair of jeans, flannel shirt, and cowboy hat. She ran to him and wrapped her arms around him in a tight embrace. "You're here!"

"Sweetheart. Are you okay?" He gently pulled back to look at her.

"Dad, it's really you. I can't believe we're here...together! You're the reason I took this journey."

"Journey?"

"Where were you?" Mia wiped tears from her eyes.

"I've just been tending to the crops. What are you doing out here in the fields?"

"No, listen to me. You left when I was six. But then I found your truck in the forest and set out to find you and —"

"The forest? My truck is right here. We had breakfast together this morning. Don't you remember?"

Wherever *here* was, Mia realized it wasn't her actual past. It was a version of reality where her dad had never left.

"I'm sorry I'm not making any sense. It's been a really long day. I'm just glad to see you."

He scratched his head, offsetting his cowboy hat. "I'm the one whose been looking for you. Want to ride into town with me?"

She glanced to the dirt driveway and her heart jumped at the sight of his white truck. The same one she found rusted and covered in vines in the real world. "I'd love to, Dad."

She climbed in the passenger side and breathed in the scent of wood and pipe smoke as his weathered hands took the wheel. They rode on the old farm road that she'd been down a thousand times. Dust chased after the truck. "I thought you might be getting ready for the homecoming dance. Isn't that tonight?"

She looked at the floorboard. "I'm not going."

He put a hand on her knee. "I'm sorry, sweetheart."

"Brandon backed out today. I think he's more interested in the new girl."

"Any guy would be lucky to have you as his date."

"No one thinks that, Dad."

"Well that's not entirely true, sweetheart." He always offered such kind words. They made her feel better even when she knew they weren't true. "Where are we going?"

"I thought we could eat supper at the Yellow Rose Diner and then run by the hardware store."

Mia loved being with her father, but this was surreal. This had been the worst day of her teenage years. But from the moment he appeared, the story was changing. It was as if her past was being rewritten in new ways.

She enjoyed the view as they traveled the back roads. He told her a joke she hadn't heard in years. It was corny and perfect. She had so many questions but was content to just be in his presence. That satisfied her soul more than any answers could.

Looking out the passenger window, she saw the diner's neon sign against the moon-lit sky. They pulled into the gravel parking lot and found a parking space near the front door. Mia's dad turned the ignition off but didn't move to get out of the truck.

"I picked up a little something for you." He leaned over and popped open the glove box. He reached in and handed her what looked like a small book wrapped in brown paper.

"Can I open it now?"

He smiled and nodded. She slowly un-wrapped the paper to reveal a leather journal. She started to cry.

"What's wrong, sweetheart?"

"Nothing. This is perfect."

He chuckled. "Well then what are the tears for?"

"Because this is all I want. But it isn't going to last."

"Sure it will."

"I wish it could." She flipped through the pages of the journal. She turned to the first page. The inscription on the inside cover read, "With you always. Love, Dad." She brushed a tear from her eye.

"We get to fill this out together. You and me. Road trips in this old truck. Watching our favorite movies. Finding the perfect burger joint. Every blank page means another adventure."

"That sounds wonderful, Dad. I love being with you no matter what we do. I have since I was a girl."

"You're still my girl." He squeezed her hand. He pulled a piece of paper from his shirt pocket and slid it within the pages. "Every book needs a bookmark." He winked at her.

She laughed. "You hear that?"

"What?"

"Your stomach. It's growling big time."

"Then I reckon we best eat." He walked to Mia's side of the truck and opened her door. She hopped out and tucked the small journal in the back pocket of her jeans.

They entered the diner and memories flooded Mia. This is where she'd eaten with her father every Saturday as a girl. The plastic red booths were filled with people she knew from childhood. No one had aged. Elderly couples and young families were talking about the local football team and town gossip. Waitresses were balancing trays with milkshakes.

She slid into the nearest booth and turned her attention to the menu. "Will it be just you, hon?" a waitress in a beehive hairdo asked.

Mia looked around. "My dad . . ."

"Is that him?" The waitress pointed to the jukebox across the diner where her father was bent over the neon machine. He turned and smiled as her favorite song began to play.

Holding her gaze, he approached the booth. "Seeing that this is homecoming and all, I was hoping maybe I could have this dance."

Someone had invited her to dance. Her father.

She stepped out and they stood facing each other. The folks in the diner looked up momentarily, then went back to their conversations. He put one hand on the small of her back and held her other hand firmly near his shoulder. Together, they shuffled their feet to the song. He whispered in her ear that she would always be his girl. How proud he was of her. And how beautiful she was.

She wished this moment could last forever.
But she knew it wouldn't. She wasn't sixteen
and her dad wasn't still on the farm. The past
was the past. Yet maybe this moment could
change the future. With her hand on his shoulder, she leaned back to see his eyes.

"Dad, can I ask you a really big question?"

"Sure, sweetheart. Anything."

"Do you know what we're in right now?"

He smiled. "I think we're in a diner."

Mia watched his eyes carefully. "Do you
know a woman named Iona?"

He paused. "The name sounds familiar. Is
she a friend of yours?"

"You would have met her more than two
decades ago."

"I don't understand."

"This diner, this dance, this night . . . I wish
it were all real. I miss you so much. I wish our
lives had gone this way. But this never happened in the real world. This is just a Story."

"This isn't a story, Mia. It's as real as I am."

"But you—I mean, I . . ." She sighed. "Can
we go back to our table? I want to show you
something."

They slid into the red vinyl booth, across

from each other. He took a sugar packet from the holder and slid it back and forth on the table. Then put it back. He picked up the menu, opened it, closed it, and then set it down.

"You seem restless, Dad."

"Do I? I guess I'm just hungry–"

"Then let's order."

He laughed. "I'm talking about another kind of hunger, sweetheart. About dreams that keep me up at night. I want more. For me. For us."

"There is more, Dad." She pulled the vial out of her pocket. "Do you know what this is?"

He took the container with the pearl-like finish in his weathered hand and turned it back and forth. She closed her eyes. Maybe Iona had given him similar vials for his journey. If this could jog his memory, maybe it would some-how change the course of their future.

He took the cork off and looked inside. "An empty container?"

"Yes. But it doesn't stay empty. Think Dad. Please try to remember."

He held the vial in front of his mouth like a microphone and tapped it. "Is this on?" He winked at her. "Ladies and gentleman. Never before has this diner had such a beautiful woman on the dance floor."

She grinned. Her dad held the makeshift microphone, but now spoke with a soft tenderness. "I love being your dad. I love spending time with you. Just us. Together."

He reached for the cork on the table.

"Wait. Don't put that—"

He sealed the vial and handed it to her. Her dad grinned. "Now your vial isn't empty. It's filled with my words!"

She felt a rush of cold air around them. Something was shifting. "No, no, no."

"It's okay, sweetheart. I was just trying to make you smile."

The diner rippled before her. She grabbed his hand. "I can't lose you again."

"Mia, what's happening? Where are you—"

But it was too late. The vial was satisfied. Wind rustled as the diner blurred and faded. The last thing she saw was her father's strong hands in hers.

the shift
to with

STAY *WITH* GOD

Mia long wondered what happened to her father. And then, through Story, they are reunited.

Mia's father gives her a blank journal, inviting her into adventures for just the two of them. God gives us a similar invitation. There are so many things He wants to reveal to us and initiate in us. But the pages will remain blank until we experience them together.

Whether we realize it or not, our entire life has revolved around our longing for God. It's not that He's hiding and we have to find him. He has always been with us. It's that we continually try to find contentment in other things when He is the only source that will ever satisfy.

With God, the priority is always presence over performance, intimacy over independence.

> With God, the priority is always presence over performance, intimacy over independence.

Moses so desired God's presence that he refused to lead the Israelites without Him. The wise prophet told God he'd rather call the entire trip off than do it alone (Exodus 33). Imagine if we took the same approach, not entering into any project or adventure without Him. Not out of obligation or duty, but simply because we crave His presence more than our plans.

Better than a leather journal, God gives us Himself.

steadfast

Mia sat in the elevator, unsure what just happened and unready to move forward.

The vial from the diner was in her lap. The time with her dad in his truck and the diner seemed so real. If only it was. If only he had been with her all these years. But . . . he hadn't. That's what was real.

She was back in the jacket and clothes she wore prior to the diner. She touched her teeth. No braces. Her hand went to the jacket pocket. The leather pouch was there. She opened it and set the three filled vials next to the one on her lap.

She looked at the four distinct containers. The vials were satisfied. But she wasn't. She wouldn't be until she found her father. She put them in the pouch and then secured it in her jacket pocket. Floor 5 was the top level of the brownstone. Whatever her final destination was, this would take her to it. She pushed the button, exhausted and yet excited to conclude this trip.

"Level 4 complete. Going up."

I'm not going to miss that voice.

The elevator rose and the door creaked partially open. The scent of manure filled the space. Before her was a massive barn. The sounds and smells reminded her of the family farm.

She rocked the metal door back and forth until she could squeeze through. She stepped onto a straw-covered plank wood floor. The barn was the length of a basketball court, with huge oak beams along the ceiling and a row of stalls on both sides. A man wearing a cowboy hat, boots, and a leather duster tended to one of the animals in the last stall to the right. His back was to her.

Her heart quickened. "Dad?"

He turned and took off his cowboy hat. It was Ryder.

She tried to conceal her disappointment as she walked to him.

"It's good to see you, Mia." He set the horse brush on the bench. Inside the stall, a large white horse had been saddled. It snorted and scratched at the floor with its front right hoof.

"Did you ride horses as a girl?"

"Not after I was six. My mom sold them after my Dad left." She stood in silence for a minute. "Ryder, I saw him on the last level. It was so . . . perfect."

"I'm glad you had that time together. Even if only within Story."

"Did you ever meet my dad when he was here? His name was—" She caught herself. "His name *is* Jonathan."

"He wasn't here, Mia. This is your Story."

"But when he was in the desert, did you—"

"There are as many deserts as there are Stories. And almost as many Watchmen."

"But Iona—"

"She is a Guardian."

"What does she guard? She's been no help in my journey."

"Iona has an uncanny ability to sense when a person is ready for this journey. Hers is a mission of the heart. It is not easy to usher others from their current reality into their Story . . . as you know. Once here, the Watchmen help them navigate it."

She looked at the stalls on either side of the barn. "What are the horses for?"

"These magnificent beasts are stallions." He smiled. "They belong to me. Being around these soulful animals soothes my heart and mind. This," he spread his hands, "is my refuge, a place of healing."

"I can see why you love being here." She leaned against a wood beam and sighed.

"What's troubling you, Mia?"

"Asher told me my father had been in the desert but didn't last as long as me." She looked at the mighty rafters, tears welling up. "Is that true?"

Ryder took off his duster and exited the horse stall. He stood next to Mia. "I'll share what Iona has told me. Your father was driving to a local farmer's market all those years ago when he had a flat tire. He knocked on her door for help. Somehow, she seems to know when folks are arriving before they do."

Mia thought of the meal Iona had prepared

for her and gave a knowing smile.

Ryder continued. "Iona sensed his restlessness. His desire for more. So after a long conversation, she invited him into Story." He frowned. "Somewhere along the way, things went wrong. In the desert, Asher convinced him that you were in danger. He begged Asher to get him back to the real world. But it doesn't work that way. The results are disastrous when we give the enemy power to guide or interpret our Stories."

"You mean this all happened to him because he was trying to help his daughter?"

"He was a kind man, Mia. But he trusted the wrong person . . . the one who sought to destroy him. And he hadn't faced his own Story yet. We must allow ourselves to be rescued before we try to rescue others."

"Iona gave me similar advice." She took a breath. "Ryder, is my father dead?"

A black bird flew into the stalls and landed on a rafter. Mia gasped. It was O'Neal.

She looked at Ryder. "It's the raven from my nightmare." From the beam, his shrill voice echoed in the barn. "Still alone. Always alone." The raven spread his wings and dove straight at her.

"Look out!" Ryder shouted. Mia ran. The raven screeched as it landed on her back. Sharp talons cut through her jacket into her skin. Mia threw herself back into a wall, smashing the raven into the wood. The stallions snorted and shook their manes in agitation as the enraged bird flew past them and landed on a beam above their heads.

A glow began to radiate within Ryder's arms. The light grew brighter within his scars until it crisscrossed his skin like a golden web of armor. "How dare you invade this sanctuary," he yelled at the bird.

The raven glared at Mia, then circled for a second pass. He was inches from her face when Ryder flung his arm in the bird's direction. A beam of golden light hit O'Neal, knocking him against a stall. Black feathers fluttered to the ground as the raven squawked, reoriented himself, and flew out of the barn.

Ryder's glow dimmed. He turned to Mia. "That felt good. I doubt he'll try another attack here, but the enemy clearly hasn't stopped hunting you. You must go now."

"But I've filled all the vials. I thought that meant my Story was done."

"The vials were preparation, more like the introduction to your Story. The Blue Door has always been your goal."

The blue door felt like a hazy memory. "But the elevator only goes to this level."

He smiled. "What comes next will require a bit more horsepower than an elevator." He patted the white stallion's side and motioned to Mia.

She looked from him to the stallion. "No way, Ryder. I know what you're thinking. But I'm not getting on that wild animal."

"I handpicked Steadfast especially for your journey. I know you haven't been on a horse since you were a girl. But you *can* ride this stallion. The only question is, do you want to ride?"

"Can't some vial just transport me to where I need to go? I don't trust my ability to do this."

"Trust his ability rather than yours. He knows the way. He can hear, smell, and see far better than humans. Stallions are independent and untamed. They are drawn to freedom."

Mia saw her father's face from the diner, laughing and full of life. She nodded before she realized what she was doing.

Ryder opened the stall door. Neither Mia nor the stallion moved. The magnificent beast watched her with his large brown eyes. He reared his head back and whinnied. She jumped.

"It's okay," Ryder whispered. Mia was unsure if he said that to calm her or Steadfast.

Then something shifted. The stallion bowed its head and approached her. Mia held her open palm to him. He nudged his wet nose into the hand Asher had cut. She ran her fingers through his thick mane.

"See, you're friends already."

"What if I fail?"

"The stakes are high. You may fail. But don't fail to try."

She took a deep breath. "Let's do this before I change my mind." Ryder handed her a pair of riding boot and gloves. After putting them on, she placed her right foot in the stirrup and, with one hand on Ryder, raised up until she was in the saddle. He led Steadfast out of the barn, then gave the reins a tug and the stallion paused.

"Mia, let me see the vials."

Keeping her balance on the saddle, she took the containers from the pouch and handed them to him one at a time. The first contained sparkling ocean water. The next one held the swirling scents of the bohemian kitchen. The gold energy of kintsugi pulsated in the third. In the last vial, the words of a father's love for his daughter.

He held each before Steadfast's snout, letting the stallion sniff them.

"Why are you doing that?"

"The vials contain immense power. They will provide Steadfast with the coordinates for your journey."

As the stallion took in each scent, Ryder returned that vial to Mia. She placed them back in the pouch and then tucked it safely in her jacket pocket. "So how far is this blue door?"

"It isn't like that. The door isn't bound to a single location because no one's Story happens in the same way."

"Then how will I find it?"

He put his cowboy hat back on. "It will find you... when you are ready."

"Can you come with me?"

"The Creator goes before you, preparing the way. And I will be watching. But this is your journey, Mia."

The stallion lifted his head and neighed, eager to be in the wide-open field. They heard cawing and looked to the sky. A flock of ravens circled above.

"What about them?"

"Stay focused on what's ahead. You can't ride to your destiny looking backward."

Ryder whispered in Steadfast's ear and the stallion broke into a gallop. Mia held tight to the reins but released any illusion of control over such a powerful, intelligent animal. The wind danced through Steadfast's mane as his hooves sprayed sand and stone.

With ravens following overhead, they sped through the field in search of the Blue Door.

the shift
to with

DO YOU WANT TO RIDE?

It all comes down to this. Do you want to ride?

My guess is the conversation might go something like this.

> *God:* Do you want to ride?
>
> *Us:* It depends. Where are we going?
>
> *God:* You'll see.
>
> *Us:* Can you guarantee we'll get there safely? And that it will go well once we do?
>
> *God:* The only guarantee is we'll go together. Do you want to ride?
>
> *Us:* Silence. Feet shuffle. Eyes down.

We want a guarantee before we commit. A friend of mine starts every movie by watching the last scene first. She'll enter the story only after knowing it ends well. This used to really bother me. It ruins everything to peek at the last page or scene. But then I realized she just wanted to know if she could trust the storyteller. She refused to enter any story without that assurance.

God rarely gives us upfront guarantees. He seems to prefer inviting us into adventures that include equal parts faith and mystery.

God rarely gives us upfront guarantees. He seems to prefer inviting us into adventures that include equal parts faith and mystery. Admitting you don't have all the answers just means you see the world as something to experience rather than control. New ideas and greater intimacy are only possible when we retain a sense of childlike wonder.

Leaders who forget to be students eventually calcify. If you're convinced you already have all the answers and are generally the smartest person in the room, you have little opportunity to learn, grow, or be surprised. And little use for faith.

Yet how often do we approach our own story that way? The demand for upfront answers treats God as some sort of cosmic magic eight ball. The priority shifts from intimacy during the journey to a demand for information before we will even begin the journey.

If you're convinced you already have all the answers and are generally the smartest person in the room, you have little opportunity to learn, grow, or be surprised. And little use for faith.

Years ago, my wife and I faced one of the biggest decisions of our lives. A ministry in Colorado invited me to join their team. It would involve a cross-country relocation and saying bye to a twenty-year publishing career, a fantastic church, best friends, a stellar school, and the home we raised our children in. The salary was good but quite a bit less than my corporate paycheck. On paper, the decision to pass was a no-brainer. But we didn't want to rely on human wisdom. We hungered for revelation. "God, we need a clear 'yes' before we commit. Or a solid 'no' and we'll forget about it."

Instead, He provided countless small stirrings and hints that we were to move. I pushed hard for clarity. "Come on, God. Don't be coy. Do we go or stay? One word from You will resolve this entire issue."

God offered something even greater . . . a vision that transformed our interpretation of the opportunity and of Him. With eyes closed in prayer, I saw my wife and I walking along a forest trail. We came to a clearing with a small corral. Inside were two stallions. An old rancher stood on the opposite side with a boot propped on the rail, his cowboy hat slightly cocked. When he smiled, the skin creased around his steel-blue eyes.

In this vision, God had gone before us and taken care of every detail. The path in the woods had been cleared. The horses in the corral were saddled. The gate was unlocked.

The rancher asked in a gentle voice, "Do you want to ride?" His tone conveyed respect and the promise of initiation. Had the rancher instead grabbed a megaphone and shouted "Yes, do it!" or "No, don't go!" it would have been more clear . . .

and less satisfying. Instead of quick answers, He offered deep questions. Then He graciously gave us the freedom to choose.

It took the right question for us to know our answer was a passionate *yes*. Only after we accepted the invitation did we realize there was a third horse in the stable. The offer was never to ride alone, but *with* Him.

So how did things turn out? Four years later, we still have many questions. But we've discovered answers can be overrated. Our family loves the spaciousness of our faith and life but financially, things are not so spacious. We miss the close friends and church we left behind. If my wife and I could step into a time machine, would we return to the lives we had prior to the move? We discussed that pretend option recently and agreed we'd destroy the time machine rather than lose who we have become by saying *yes* to God's invitation. We are now content to embrace this life of mystery even with the unanswered questions.

God longs for those who will come alongside Him

and experience the active, unpredictable, intimate joy of riding together. Doing so requires us to stay close. Sometimes He'll ride by our side. Other times, He leads the charge. And occasionally He falls back a bit just to see if we notice. It's how a good father trains children to ride.

After spending time in her Story, Mia knows the only hope of finding her father is to ride. She doesn't have all the answers, but if the choice is to pursue life with or without her father, she chooses with.

We each face a similar decision. Do we hunger more for guarantees . . . or God?

options

The flock of ravens looked like black specks peppering the sky. The formation moved with them, silently following.

Mia was staring at them when Steadfast abruptly stopped.

Twenty feet ahead, the cliff dropped several hundred feet straight down. Mia stroked the stallion's thick neck, thankful they hadn't gone over the edge while she was distracted. But why would Steadfast bring her to this dead end?

The ravens hovered, awaiting their next move. She spun Steadfast around back the way they had come. Then one raven shot from the sky straight toward them. Hundreds of the birds joined, forming a living black wall of wings that blocked their escape.

Mia glanced to her left. No way to ride through the dense forest growth. On the right, a mountain wall rose straight up. Behind her, the edge of the cliff. They were boxed in.

It was impossible to get around the birds as they flew forward, prodding Mia and Steadfast to back up. Each step took them closer to the edge. The stallion shook his head and Mia tugged at the reins. A few feet more and they'd fall over the side.

From where Steadfast now stood, Mia could see a small opening in the wall of rock. It was narrow, but wide enough for them to make it through . . . if they could dart to the right before the ravens could reposition themselves. If the birds suddenly attacked, Steadfast might panic. And a misstep would be a step off the cliff. She had to act now.

Mia leaned down and whispered into his right ear. "Take us into the cave." Then she prodded Steadfast with her right heel and he bolted to the opening. Caught off guard, the birds scattered as Mia and Steadfast raced into the crevice.

Once inside the cool cavern walls, Mia realized there would be no way for the stallion to maneuver in the tight confines ahead. She lowered herself from the saddle, stroked his side, and said softly, "Be free, my friend." He brushed his nose against her hand, then turned around. He sped from the cave and Mia heard the ravens screech as he charged through them and down the trail.

Without Steadfast, Mia could make her way through the tight spaces easier. Yet the farther in she went, the darker it became. She held her arms before her so she wouldn't run into anything. The walls of the tunnel twisted and gradually narrowed at each turn.

"Still running, Mia?" A chill ran down her spine at the sound of Asher's voice behind her. "I must warn you, there's no way out. You are trapped."

The sides of Mia's shoulders now touched the cavern walls. As she proceeded, the space and even the air were thinner. Sweat coated her entire body.

"I could send my ravens after you. You wouldn't see them coming in the dark. But they'd see you."

She remembered the nightmare of the ravens attacking her. Then put it out of her mind. Her only option was to keep moving forward, though she now had to turn sideways to squeeze through the pitch-black tunnel. If only she had a flashlight.

Wait. Maybe she did. She pulled the pouch from her jacket pocket. The blue *Identity* vial still danced with the light of kintsugi. She held up the container, using its luminous gold glow to navigate the passageway.

"Thanks for the light," Asher called out. "It will draw the ravens to you like moths to a flame." The tunnel began to widen. Mia no longer had to turn sideways. A feeling of hope surged through her as she entered the wide open space. She held the vial high. The light revealed a cavern the size of a large room. Then her chest tightened. There was no way out.

Mia spoke softly to the Creator. "I'm stuck in a cave with my enemy closing in. Please don't let me die."

Silence.

"I'm not picky. Forget the Blue Door. I'll settle for any door that gets me out of here!"

Seven doors of various shapes and sizes suddenly materialized along the cavern walls. All were blue. Mia was stunned. Iona had only mentioned one door. But maybe the Creator chose to provide her with multiple ways out.

She had to move fast; Asher and his ravens couldn't be far behind. Mia held the kintsugi vial high as she approached the first option. She turned the knob and opened the door. It was some kind of portal. Behind it was the gentleman from Strava who dismissed her earlier. He stood in the conference room facing her. "Thanks for coming back, Mia. We made an enormous mistake. The position is yours . . . if you want it."

She took one step forward, then hesitated. What if one of the other six doors offered an even better option? "Give me one minute! I may be back." She closed the door. She moved to the next one and opened it. Her mother stood before her in an apron, holding a slice of pink cake. "Mia, I love your cake. You are an incredible cook, just like your dad." Mia slammed the door in her face, which would infuriate her mom . . . if that really was her mom. Either way, there had to be a better option.

The next door had a rounded top and was ocean blue. It reminded her of being in the water with Shay. She recalled his words about actively waiting for the right wave instead of trying to make her own. She paused. Mia realized she was racing from door to door, like a game-show contestant looking for the best prize.

She stopped. "I don't know what to do. You show me the right door."

"Are you asking me for help?" Asher appeared, holding a torch. The cavern grew bright with the flame.

"You're too late, Asher. I've found the Blue Door."

"I see seven of them. Better choose carefully." He propped the torch upright between two rocks.

She hesitated. Her only escape was through one of the doors, but which one? Or did it matter? She asked the Creator for an open door and multiple ones appeared. Maybe it was her choice.

Last time she faced Asher, he talked her into trying to overcome the desert in her own strength. Not this time. She closed her eyes and turned her attention fully to the Creator.

"Which door is the right one?"

Focus on Me, not the doors.

The voice was so real, Mia felt sure some-one else had entered the cavern. But only Asher was there.

He mocked her as he grew closer with each step. "Is this the right door? Then again, maybe it's this one?"

Mia tried to focus on the Creator as the enemy neared.

"How do I do this?" she whispered.

With Me.

The vial in her hand began to shake. The glow of the kintsugi intensified, highlighting the etched word *Identity* on the container. She remembered her promise in the desert. "I will do this as Your daughter."

Asher was a few feet from her. He snick-ered. "His daughter? The Creator doesn't want you. You're damaged goods."

Fury shot through Mia. "You're a liar!" She threw the vial at Asher's head. He ducked and it shattered against the door behind him, releasing golden liquid over the entire surface.

The door flickered before being overcome by the light. Then it was gone.

She stared in disbelief. The vials weren't just her way up. They were her way out. All she had to do was free what was inside.

"What are you doing?" Asher roared. She saw a hint of fear flash across his face.

As Mia reached for the leather pouch with the other three containers, Asher thrust a hand toward her. "You have no idea what you're unleashing."

"You're right," she said holding the container of ocean water, "but I am . . . expectant." She flung the *Expectant* vial at a door just past Asher. He reached for it but missed. The tube broke and glistening water drizzled down the blue wood. The door shimmered for a second, then vanished.

Asher glared at her. "This ends now."

"Not yet." She now had the *Awaken* vial from the bohemian kitchen. "Let's see what this cooks up." He charged at her. Before she could throw it, he grabbed her arm. The container fell to the cave floor. As it burst open, the smell of fresh baked bread filled the enclosed cavern. Another door stretched, faded, and disappeared. Four remained.

She tried to jerk her right arm free but he

refused to let go. The last vial, the one from the diner, was in her left hand.

"You're destroying every door. Keep this up and the real one will be gone too."

"I'm not looking for an open door. I'm looking for Him."

His face inches from hers, he spoke through gritted teeth. "You have some real father issues, Mia. The Creator doesn't want you as a daughter. Even your dad left when you were a girl. But trust me," he sneered, "that was no big loss. Your dad was nothing special."

"No one says that about my father." She took a step toward him, then looked down and bit her lower lip.

"What are you going to do, slap me?"

Her left hand clenched into a fist, the vial inside it. She then thrust her hand at Asher's face, opening it palm out at the last second. The vial smashed into his nose, knocking his glasses off. The shattered shards of glass embedded into his skin. He screamed in pain and covered his face, releasing her wrist as he did. The leather pouch in her palm kept her hand from being cut.

Freed from the vial, her father's words reverberated through the cavern.

"Mia, I love being your dad." It was his voice from the diner. The vial had held them for this moment.

One of the remaining four blue doors began to convulse against the force of her dad's words. Then disappeared.

Asher looked up, blood on his face.

Tears welled in Mia's eyes as her dad's words filled the cave. "I love spending time with you."

Another door imploded.

Her father's voice continued. "Just us."

A blue door grew smaller and smaller until it was no more.

"Together."

The last door crumbled into splinters of blue wood.

Asher stood in stunned silence. Then he started to clap slowly. "Bravo, Mia. In your brilliance, you destroyed every blue door. You now have no way out."

She heard the rustle of wings and saw dozens of ravens enter the cavern. They landed on the rocks and stared at her, their eyes glowing from the torch flame.

Mia's shoulders slumped. This made no sense. Weren't the vials supposed to lead her to the Blue Door, not destroy them all?

Light the darkness, Mia.

She whispered. "I don't understand, Father. There are no more vials."

You light it.

Suddenly a flicker began to glow from the scar in her palm. She held her arm high and a luminous ribbon of gold flowed up and down the crevices and cracks of the cave walls until the darkness was overcome with the liquid light of kintsugi.

Asher seemed afraid of the light. He retreated to where the ravens gathered.

Like an electric current, the kintsugi flowed through the cavern. When it came to the place where the ocean water had splashed against the cave wall, sparks ignited and the glow grew even brighter. Then it fused with the swirling scent of the bohemian kitchen and the words of her father. As the four elements became one, the glowing gold transformed into shimmering blue liquid light. It slid down the cavern wall, spreading the blue until it covered a rectangular area of the rock. The light grew so intense that she had to shield her eyes.

When she could see again, a translucent

blue door was now fused into the cavern wall. But unlike any of the previous doors, this was a truer blue than she had ever seen, as if everything blue in this world was just a pale imitation of what the Creator originally meant when he made the color blue. The door had a rough silver knob, like the metal had been beaten with a hammer. The door's shimmering cobalt surface wasn't metal or wood. It seemed to be alive and shifted with the light, made from a material unknown in our reality.

This was the Blue Door that Iona spoke of. Not one born from desperation but from an expectant spirit, an awakened heart, a true identity, and her Father's voice. She realized the previous doors were Asher's creations. As long as she just wanted an open door, he was happy to help. Anything to distract her from discovering the one true door.

Mia turned the silver knob and opened the door. The other side was bathed in a cool blue light. Without a look back, she walked through. It felt like she had entered water, but the shimmering blue before her wasn't wet.

In the dazzling presence of the Creator, she had forgotten about Asher and the ravens. But now they charged at her. She tensed, ready for the force of their assault. But they slammed into an invisible barrier at the door's frame. The raging birds were inches from Mia, but might as well have been in another dimension.

She locked eyes with Asher. Dried blood was on his face. "The Blue Door can only be entered *with* the Creator," she said with a new-found authority. "Though you taunt those in this realm and try to steal their true identity, you are the one who has chosen to oppose the Creator. And that makes you the only true Orphan."

He beat his fists against the clear barrier but couldn't get to Mia.

The atmosphere on this side of the Blue Door was so intoxicating that it was impossible to focus on him any longer. He was like a gnat vying for attention in the presence of the Grand Canyon.

Without a backward glance, she closed the Blue Door, and stepped forward into freedom.

the shift
to with

OPEN AND CLOSED DOORS

Appearing to be out of options, Mia screams in frustration, "Forget the Blue Door." She'll settle for any door that gets her out of the dire situation.

Can you relate? We face so many closed doors in our lives. We long for an open door. Any open door. Yet we will misinterpret so much if we assume every open door must be from God. Send out three applications for three jobs and one company responds positively. It must be a sign from God, right? The same with closed doors. We pursue our passion but hit a dead end. So we shrug our shoulders and assume God must be the one who closed that door.

The problem is we have an enemy who opens and closes doors too. Remember, Asher didn't care which door Mia went through as long as it kept her from the one that led to true freedom.

As Ryder said, "The door will find you when you are ready." It wasn't until Mia focused on the Creator rather than a door (or answer) that things began to shift.

As Mia discovered through the vials, we learn about God not just by facts and lessons, but also through our senses. He is the God of colors, music, flowers, sunsets, words, and food. He invites us to see, hear, touch, and taste that He is good. That is why each vial contained a sensory element that when combined, revealed the way forward.

There is no lock on the Blue Door. Which means there isn't some key that only a few have access to. Yet there's an endless line of people who promise that they have discovered the secret to success. All we need to do is master their ten steps and surely that key will work for us as well.

> He is the God of colors, music, flowers, sunsets, words, and food. He invites us to see, hear, touch, and taste that He is good.

Except it almost certainly won't. Because no one has *the* key or secret. If they did, we'd know it by now. But the pull is magnetic. The gatekeepers of certain industries position themselves as the ultimate decision makers of careers and trends. The problem is that industry experts only offer industry answers. And those answers are almost always based on what worked in the past. In other words, they offer reactive responses and educated guesses while God invites His children into a future that surpasses human limitations or expectations. When we only consider the options we know are possible, we miss the higher options of God.

When you face big decisions, can you rest with God in the unknown or do you immediately gravitate to a "pros and cons" list, adding up the columns to determine your best option? That process feels logical, but it can "con" us because the choices are limited to our best thinking in the moment. Where we see three possible options, God sees endless possibilities. But He will leave us to our three if we refuse to invite Him into the process. Thankfully, He stands ready to share His higher options once we're ready to release our best options.

The best way to proceed is always together. Which is why there is only one way for Mia to enter through the Blue Door. *With* God.

bohemians

The blue light liquid that surrounded Mia in the tunnel was surreal. It was like a balm that soothed her spirit and restored her weariness with each step. Her feet didn't seem to touch solid ground, yet she easily walked through it. The cool breeze at her back wooed her forward.

She couldn't see too far ahead because the passageway curved every fifteen feet or so, but she could hear distant voices. She walked at an easy pace, expectant that something good was ahead. The intoxicating scent of peony and the presence of fireflies added a sense of wonder to this part of her journey.

It was hard to gauge how long she'd been in the tunnel, but eventually she heard music and laughter. As she moved forward, the smell of roasting meat wafted through the air. The anticipation of what awaited her was almost too much.

And then she was there.

As she stepped out of the passageway, her eyes grew wide. Before her was a rooftop party. While there were more than a hundred people present, the gathering had an intimate vibe with small groups of people everywhere. Wooden cabanas provided a place to linger and connect. Chinese lanterns and tiki torches brought just enough light without diminishing the stars above. Waitstaff roamed the floor with trays of food and drink. The energy was kinetic and palpable.

Mia was mesmerized by the diversity of attendees. Some dressed for a night on the town. Others wore shorts and sandals. Some came in attire that applied to their calling, from a coach to a barista. As Mia wandered, she caught bits of conversation. Buzz over a new screenplay. A cappella singing. Talk of a new recipe. A robust conversation about what makes a hero.

Each area on the roof had its own personality. To her right, people clustered in casual conversation. Straight ahead, people relaxed on overstuffed couches in an eclectic lounge. Farther away, people danced to an instrumental band. She thought of the dance with her father at the diner. If only he could be with her now.

"Mia, you made it!"

She turned to see the most stunning woman. The simple black dress made her silver hair even more striking.

"Iona!" She ran to her and the two embraced. "You were right. Everything you said. Thank you."

"I simply invited you into your Story. You lived it well. And this . . . what do you think?"

"Where is 'this', Iona?"

"We're on the roof of the brownstone."

"But this space is so much larger than the building we were in."

Iona grinned. "Is it larger than oceans and deserts? We are in a place of abundance, remember? The atmosphere can't help but expand for such a gathering. Before us are poets, architects, singers, painters, writers, dancers, teachers, actors, athletes, and chefs. Some create works of art while others create space for people to discover their calling. Around us are rare ones of every talent who have braved the levels necessary to make it through the Blue Door."

"But my father. Is he here?"

Iona's disposition changed. "Mia, I'm glad you had time with your father in the Story. But he isn't here."

Mia looked down. "The reason I agreed to this was to find him."

"Yet you found your own Story instead."

"I am a changed woman. But after seeing a version of my dad at the diner, I can't help but believe he's still out there. Maybe he's lost his Story, but he's alive. I can feel it."

"Hold on to that, Mia. But don't miss what is before you." Iona led her across the rooftop in silence. A breeze blew through the star-dusted sky as they paused to take in the gentle strum of a guitar. The woman's chords echoed with sound but also with light and color. A few feet away, a sketch artist brought his canvas to life one stroke at a time. His drawing seemed to shift, the paper unable to hold the charcoal image captive. On the far end of the roof, a volleyball game with a glow-in-the-dark ball was in progress. "I love how everyone here is so . . . different."

"Creative fellowship doesn't mean creative sameness. The common bond is that these people share the desire to pursue their lives and their gifts with the Creator."

A burley chef scurried past them. Mia did a double take.

"Chef Gino?" She bent down to give the small chef a big hug.

"You are alive!" he exclaimed."If I ever see that troublemaker again, I will–"

"That troublemaker turned out to be my rescuer."

The chef's eyes widened. "It is a very strange Story we find ourselves in, is it not?"

"Yes, but also a beautiful one. Like the time in your kitchen." She looked at Iona, then back at the chef. "What are you doing here?"

He raised a finger. "This is the event we were preparing for this morning."

Had it really only been earlier that day when they met? It felt like a lifetime ago, but as Iona implied, experiences within Story are not bound by something as fragile and finite as time.

"Are Celtic Chef and Bandana here too?"

"But of course. We don't just pursue our love of food together. We get to witness the joy people experience with our creations. You cannot be part bohemian and part orphan. True success means you create *with* the Creator, in fellowship *with* others, as you engage *with* the community your creation serves. With. With. With."

He realized he was still balancing a tray of drinks. "Please sample. I call this my Peppermint Swirl Infusion."

"This looks like a work of art," Mia said as she took a glass.

"Do not admire. Drink!" He winked and then bustled away.

Mia sipped the swirled infusion. It was delicious.

The lights suddenly dimmed across the roof, leaving only the glow of candles, moon, and stars.

"It is about to begin," Iona said.

"What is?"

"The Feast of the Brave."

the shift
to with

CREATIVE FELLOWSHIP

Mia spent her entire life believing she was all on her own. Then she entered a truer Story and realized she had never been alone. God was always with her.

On the rooftop, she stepped into another awakening, the knowledge that our Story grows even richer with the presence of others.

Mia got her first taste of this in Chef Gino's kitchen. Now she has encountered a rooftop filled with others who hunger and thirst for more.

Bohemians, according to one dictionary.com definition, are "those who live free of conventional rules and the man-made rules that limit one's creativity." The only One with unlimited creativity is God. Those at the rooftop gathering understand that we need relationship with God. And we need relationship with others. One without the other is less than what we were created for.

That's why Scripture tells us loving God and loving others are the highest priorities of our lives (Mark 12:29).

On a practical level, your creativity will soar when you surround yourself with a small

> We need relationship with God. And we need relationship with others. One without the other is less than what we were created for.

fellowship of like-minded bohemians from a variety of backgrounds. There is incredible ideation and energy that occurs when songwriters mingle with chefs. Architects gather with poets. And teachers share a meal with storytellers. A community is formed that doesn't compete but that feeds off one another and helps dreams fly higher. I'm talking about a small fellowship of friends who, depending on the moment, have permission to lift you up or pull you back down to earth.

You need a group like that and they need you. Because there's more to your Story than you and God. There's also you and others.

fog

The bohemians gathered at massive oak tables arranged in concentric circles at the center of the roof. Engraved on the back of each handcrafted chair was a person's name. No two plates or glasses were the same. Even the silverware was unique to each setting. The feast was meant to satisfy more than physical hunger. It was designed to satisfy each attendee's longing to be known.

Mia stared in wonder as stars shimmered in the evening sky. She imagined she was on top of a medieval castle, celebrating a tremendous victory. "It's like we've entered into a fairy tale."

"Indeed," Iona said looking at the gathering clouds above. "A tale of immense beauty . . . and danger." She stood and made her way to the center of the tables. A hush fell over the group.

"Welcome to the Feast of the Brave." She made eye contact with as many bohemians as possible. "Many of you spend your days at a table—whether a drafting, kitchen, classroom, or writer's table. Tonight we feast at the banquet table."

She smiled as she roamed from person to person. "Each of your lives and the creativity within you matter more than you imagine. Your presence is both desired and needed in the world."

She raised a goblet. "As a fellowship of freedom seekers, we give thanks to our Creator."

The bohemians lifted their glasses and took a long drink of the refreshing liquid. As if on cue, a dozen chefs led by Chef Gino came alongside Iona. She spread her arms wide. "The realm's top attendants are here to serve you an exquisite four-course meal. I would share the menu with you, but it varies by person based on the foods you most love. No two meals tonight will be the same. Each of you will receive a custom serving of your favorite appetizer, entrée, and dessert."

That's three courses — not four, Mia thought. Though she wasn't complaining.

"As you savor the food, your imagination will also be fed through the talents of dancers, guitar players, opera singers, and acrobats. Look into the eyes of those seated around you. Hear their stories and share yours. We gather as a fellowship to cheer each other on, to taste the diverse creativity, and to celebrate our Creator."

As Iona spoke, a dense fog crept silently across the rooftop floor like dirty water. The crowd grew distracted.

"What's going on?" a voice shouted from a table near Mia.

Iona was unshaken. "Not what, *who*. Asher is trying to disorient us. Even here, he seeks to distract us and cloud our thinking." The fog rose higher, so thick that people could barely see in front of them. Plates crashed as servers stumbled and people left their tables to escape the mist.

Iona's voice broke through the chaos. "Everyone stay calm. Resist the confusion he is trying to bring."

The inability to see anything brought an immediate sense of isolation and panic. Toxic whispers from the enemy wove through the fog, spreading fear and envy around those present.

Did you see that look earlier? She's jealous.

I have no new ideas. My best days are behind me.

Why does success come so easy for him?

There was a mistake. I'm not supposed to be here.

If they only knew my past . . .

Mia felt a wave of regret hit her as she sat in the fog. The whole reason she agreed to this journey was to find her father. She had almost died several times to accomplish her mission. But he wasn't here. She felt sure no one else here had to deal with that kind of loss. She just wanted to be by herself.

As the fog thinned, Mia found herself with just Iona on the rooftop.

"Where is everyone?"

"What thoughts ran through your mind as the fog hit?"

"That no one could understand my loss. I wanted to be alone."

Iona nodded. "And now you are. Asher knows the more unseen we feel, the more vulnerable we become. In the fog of confusion, some get hit with thoughts they are invisible or irrelevant. It's the fear of being forgotten. Or not enough. Others are tempted with a desire for independence and isolation. They often wrestle with the fear of failure."

"Where did everyone go?"

"They are still here. But we can only see what we believe to be true. And at the moment, everyone believes they are on their own."

"Can you fix it?"

Iona put her hand on Mia's shoulder. "You have the authority to fight the enemy's lies. *You* fix it."

As she spoke, a dark mist swirled around Mia. Anger rose within her. She turned her back on Iona. "You led me to believe I'd find my dad by the end of the journey. But that was a lie. Just leave me alone."

There was no response.

"Did you hear what I said?"

Mia spun around. She was alone on the roof. She shouted into the mist, "How do I push the fog back, Iona? I don't know what to do."

Yes you do. Stay with me. And resist the enemy. For yourself . . . and for others.

Mia recognized the Creator's voice. She remembered Ryder's words from the desert. And she knew what she had to do. She held her arms out in front of her. "I stand with the Creator against this attack. The enemy has no authority or power over me."

She paused. Nothing changed. So she pressed in further.

"Asher, you are banned from this rooftop. The fog of confusion must leave this gathering." It felt like slogging through molasses as she spoke those words. But as she pushed through, a soft gold glow emanated from her palm.

She took a deep breath and began. "Friends, we can't trust our eyes at this moment. It appears to each of us that we're alone. But we aren't. We are a fellowship." She stared into the fog. "I was wrong. I don't want to do this on my own. Not the pain or the celebrations. I need you. More than that, I want you by my side in this journey."

The glow from her palm grew brighter. Small rays of light ebbed from her fingertips and began to cut through the mist. Mia raised her voice. "Each of you must proclaim your identity as a son or daughter of the Creator.

Speak it aloud. Let the scars of your story be heard by others. Doing so diffuses the enemy's lies and our wounds become weapons of light."

She could hear voices within the mist. People were sharing their stories. As they did, they became visible again. Flickers of gold light shimmered and began to dismantle the fog. Ribbons of kintsugi swirled between and among the people, drawing them together.

In the fog, each person felt alone. But as it thinned, it was clear others had been near them the entire time. Mia was with an architect, dentist, barista, and high school coach. There was nothing remarkable in the appearance of anyone there . . . or in any other group. They were ordinary people she wouldn't have given a second glance to back in the real world. But here, they were titans, generals, and legends in the making. She was amazed at the journeys each braved to be on the rooftop with her. She was overcome with emotion at the countless stories of rescue and redemption.

Mia saw that Iona was there, in one of the other groups. She was listening intently, tears in her eyes. Mia moved to the middle of the gathering. "Everyone raise your arms skyward.

Father of Lights, we embrace our place here with You. Only your light and only your presence here. Let us see each other as You see us."

At that moment, luminous gold light burst forth from each person's scars. It sliced through the remaining mist. The bohemians were light bearers, beaming with the healing power of kintsugi. The scars that once separated them were now the bond that connected them.

The entire rooftop was bathed in light, outshining even the stars above them. In that moment, the bohemian gathering shifted from a festive party to a fellowship of creative warriors looking out for one another.

the shift
to with

WEAPONS OF LIGHT

Even after we step into freedom, the enemy will taunt us and try to cause us to forget our true identity. His primary strategy is to isolate us from God . . . and each other.

> The enemy will taunt us and try to cause us to forget our true identity. His primary strategy is to isolate us from God . . . and each other.

On the rooftop, in the midst of an incredible celebration, a fog rolls in and disorients the bohemians. Soon, they can no longer see each other—or what is true.

Fog often precedes the feast being prepared for us. It clouds our view of reality. Though God and others remain beside us, we lose sight of them.

What clears the fog is fellowship with God and others. And remembering who we are. We do that by proclaiming our identity as His sons and daughters. And sharing our stories with others.

In the Orphan Realm, everyone was taught to hide his or her scars. But here on the rooftop, Mia realizes the power of scars that have been redeemed. They reveal a part of each person's past rescue . . . and future glory.

God doesn't hide our broken places but transforms them. We are healed with His gold and made more unique and more us than we ever were before. And when we share the scars of our story, our wounds transform into weapons of light.

feast

"Tonight you have seen what the world calls the impossible." Iona drank deeply from her goblet before continuing. "The enemy attempted to disrupt our gathering, but he cannot stop this celebration. Everyone, please find your chair and let us continue."

A young man next to Iona asked, "But why would a party be attacked? It's not like we're doing anything dangerous here."

"Do not be deceived. What happens here is dangerous . . . for good. We're made for human fellowship. Those who believe in God but choose to live in isolation miss out on the

Feast of the Brave."

Iona motioned to the waitstaff to bring out the main course. "Tonight's meal offers a taste of what is to come. One day we will gather at the most amazing banquet ever. The book of Revelation refers to it as the Wedding Feast of the Lamb. At that time, His sons and daughters throughout history will celebrate the Creator. It will be a time of new songs, joyful dancing, epic stories, deep laughter, and restored hope."

Iona walked between the tables as she continued. "As bohemian artists, you hear, taste, and see things others don't. You breathe the eternal into existence. But only when you pursue your talent with the Creator."

The conversation continued into the evening, as one story led to another. Eventually, the chefs brought out dessert—each plate held an original creation for a specific person. There was a mix of chilled, heated, crusted, infused, fruit and chocolate creations. Some were glazed in exotic sauces. Others featured hand-picked wild berries. Celtic Chef brought Mia a slice of pink cake. Before she could take a bite, a familiar voice sounded from behind the tables.

"It is time to offer our talents to our Creator."

She spun around to see an oak of a man approach the gathering. It was Ryder! His massive frame moved to the center of the roof. Iona embraced him, then returned to her seat next to Mia.

"Welcome Bohemians, Guardians, and Watchmen." His baritone voice reverberated throughout the rooftop. "You are here because you pursue your life and creativity the same way you entered the Blue Door . . . with the Creator. The key is *with*.

Ryder let that sink in. "May everything we do be with God. Better to call your dreams off than to attempt them in your own strength. We never want our talent or fame to become an idol. So tonight, as a gathering, we offer our bodies, minds, hands, and imaginations back to the Creator — as an offering."

The bohemians stood and cheered. There was an intense desire for the Creator to fill every aspect of their minds and hearts, individually and as a group.

The Watchman lifted his muscular arms skyward. "Creator of all, we celebrate Your presence here tonight. We are free because You have broken our chains, rescued us from deserts, healed our scars, and transformed us from living as orphans to being your sons and daughters.

"You birthed in us our unique desires and passions. May the full force of all you dreamed when You created us become a reality. May our talents blaze with Your life and light. We celebrate the unique skills You have given to each of us. But more than the gifts, we celebrate You. Fame may or may not come. Help us be the same person no matter the outcome. Because either way, our reward is You. And though You may have more for us, You are more than enough. Let us be fully satisfied by You and You alone.

"We give You every aspect of our lives. May we not look to the world for inspiration or validation. It didn't give us our mission nor can it take it from us. It didn't give us our identity, so it can't tell us who we are . . . or aren't.

"We declare that the enemy has no place in our lives or in the life-giving process of creation. You are the Author of life. We resist the fog of lies that tries to derail us through isolation, distraction, despair, or disheartenment.

"With Your presence, we need never fear.

"With You, we can do the impossible.

"With You, we are never alone.

"May our creations make You smile. May You give us a glimpse of the eternal songs, stories, and images that reverberate through Your Kingdom. Let us taste those and then share that with the world. But most of all, may we never lose our hunger for Your presence.

"Tonight, we give you . . . us."

As Ryder finished, some cried, some knelt, and others danced. All were in awe of what they had just been a part of.

Mia turned to Iona. "I'm sorry for lashing out at you earlier. The fog—"

"It is okay, Mia. I know your heart."

She started to respond but was distracted by shimmering lights within the clouds. The sky opened up and stars seemed to fall to the roof in slow motion.

Ryder smiled. "I hope you saved room for the final course."

Hundreds of small, dough-like spheres no larger than a silver dollar drifted down. It was as if the entire roof were inside a slow-motion snow globe. Iona caught one in her hand and savored the smell. "Manna!"

Mia turned to her. "Like what God fed Moses and His followers in the desert?"

"Yes. Some translate manna as 'What is it?' The fact that its very name is a question prompts us to embrace mystery as we tilt our heads toward what is higher."

A piece landed in Mia's outstretched palm. She cupped it close to her face, inhaling the fragrance. The smell reminded her of the fresh baked bread from the bohemian kitchen.

"Can I eat it?"

Iona nodded. "It is for everyone who hungers for more of the Creator. It offers a taste of the eternal so we don't grow weary with the everyday."

Mia closed her eyes and ate a piece. It warmed her body and soul.

Everyone looked skyward. Some let the manna drift into their hands. Others caught the substance on their tongues. The entire roof buzzed with a sense of childlike wonder.

Ryder beamed. "The world is starving. Each of you has the ability to change the atmosphere in your circles. You have the honor of feeding those who hunger through your life, your work, and your creativity. Let that begin now."

Mia turned to Iona. "I wondered what tonight's final course would be."

"And?"

"I think the Creator outdid even Chef Gino. He saved the best for last."

the shift
to *with*

WHAT SATISFIES THE HUNGER

Imagine being at a rooftop party where you're participating in an amazing celebration of freedom and creativity. But you aren't just a random attendee. Your presence enhances the event. You don't just have a place at the table. A chair has been crafted that is the perfect fit, with your name carved into it. Those seated next to you are the very people you most want to spend time with. And your favorite meal is being prepared just for you in the kitchen.

That is the Feast of the Brave. A place to fast from tips and techniques as you feast with God and others. It is state of mind that knows God's presence never wavers—whether in times of wonder or wilderness.

In a world driven by scarcity, that may sound too good to be true. Yet the Freedom Realm is one of abundance. We have to reorient ourselves to this new atmosphere.

The enemy wants us to believe that God only offers crumbs. The Creator crumbles that lie as He satisfies our every desire with a feast of abundance. He invites us to the table, not as servants or waiters, but as part of the community. Even more, as family. Our names are permanently engraved on the chairs because the invitation is not conditional. It is based on His unconditional love for us. There is nothing we can do to lose our place at the table . . . or earn a better one.

But we will miss this fellowship if we don't frequent the table.

> We will miss this fellowship if we don't frequent the table.

Mia has always been drawn to food, and that desire has taken her from deep hunger all the way to a lavish rooftop feast. Her father inspired in her the love of cooking. But once he disappeared, her attempts to pursue this passion were met with scorn by her mother and disinterest by Strava.

In the forest, Mia shared a simple snack of apples and cheese with another orphan. Then Iona invited her to a meal where Story was the main course. From there, Mia experienced a whole new way to cook with bohemian chefs. And had a timeless conversation at a diner with her dad.

Now she finds herself at a banquet table with creative soul mates. And the culmination of that feast is manna from above, spiritual food to sustain her by reminding Mia that her Creator is also her Provider.

Whether large or small, these are the meals that will satisfy your hunger for more.

God invites you to frequent the table daily. Remember to save room for the manna.

unfinished

E ven the best gatherings must end. At least on this side of eternity.

As the crowd thinned, Mia lingered at the fire pit with Iona and Ryder. She wasn't sure how everyone else had exited the rooftop, nor was she ready to find out.

The flames flickered, casting shadows on their faces. Embers floated up, trying to join the stars above. Iona sang a Celtic ballad of times long past and times yet to be. Ryder pointed out constellations she'd never seen. And Mia shared dreams that had been brimming inside her since childhood.

Even with the fire, Mia shivered in the cool air. Ryder reached for a new piece of wood to keep the flames going. As he did, Mia noticed the scars on his arms were in odd configurations.

"The markings resemble letters."

He nodded. "Sometimes when the Creator heals my wounds, He inscribes the names of people I've helped. As a reminder."

"Am I–"

"Yes, Mia. Your name is here."

As she stared at his visible sacrifice for her, the piece of wood ignited in Ryder's left hand. He tossed the flaming log into the fire pit.

"How'd you do that?"

"You crack me up, girl. You've seen the impossible and then you're amazed when I light a piece of wood?"

She smiled as she wrapped her arms around her knees and rocked herself back and forth. "I don't want this end. Being with like-minded people in this fantastical place is exhilarating. When I leave, it will just become a memory. And that feels like another loss."

"That's why you need creative fellowship," Iona said.

"I could use a group like that."

Iona smiled. "They could use you too."

Ryder stared into the fire. "The world has grown cold. It needs the glow from those who have spent time with the Creator. It's the difference between one who warms herself by a small fire but has little to offer and a bohemian whose face is so bright from being in the Creator's presence that she doesn't need a fire to warm those around her."

"How do I do that, Ryder?"

"Don't *do* that. *Be* that. You're a different person after this journey. Approach every aspect of your life differently."

"I feel so unfinished."

"We are all unfinished," Iona said. "And that's a beautiful place to be. Unfinished means there is more. When you're finished, your story is over and done. Yours has more chapters to be written—not here, but in the real world."

"Whoa, hold on. I'm not ready to go. Not yet."

Iona and Ryder exchanged glances.

"Mia . . . ," Iona said.

"No, listen. It cost me so much to get to this rooftop. It's been the most incredible time of my life up here. Now you're just going to yank me back to the real world?"

"This isn't your home, Mia."

"I don't want to lose this place."

"You're leaving it, not losing it. The goal was never to escape the real world. But to learn how to live differently within it. The freedom you tasted here will stay with you. It is a state of mind and a place of the heart."

"But what about my father?"

"You had to find your Story before you could find him. If he's still lost, it isn't here in your Story. It's in his Story."

"I don't understand."

Ryder put his hand on her shoulder. "You will."

Tears welled in her eyes. "I know you're a Watchman. But to me, you are a kintsugi knight. Will I see you again?"

"You are tattooed on my arm, Mia. I will continue to watch over you." Ryder gave her an enormous hug. Mia collapsed into his massive arms, lingering in his embrace as long as possible.

"It is time."

Mia's hand instinctively went to the pocket on her jacket. The pouch was there but the vials were gone.

Iona pointed to her heart. "In the real world, the power of the vials is contained here. Fill your heart with those substances and it will be satisfied."

Mia took a lingering glance at the rooftop, remembering all that happened tonight. "Okay, I'm as ready as I'll ever be."

Iona reached out and they clasped hands. "Now we return. This has been a Story of ocean and desert, feast and famine, stallions and ravens, scars and healing. It is your Story, Mia. And you didn't just survive. You've found your truer self. You left the real world believing you were an orphan. You return a daughter of the Creator, never to go through life alone."

The atmosphere shifted and crackled. When Mia opened her eyes, she found herself back at the table behind Iona's home. Ice was still in their glasses. The table just as it had been during their meal. Iona sat across from her.

"Mia, can you hear me? You did it! You're home."

But nothing seemed right. And it certainly didn't feel like home.

the shift
to with

THE FREEDOM REALM

Mia got her first taste of the Freedom Realm at the rooftop gathering. And it surpassed anything she could have imagined.

She was in a place of kindred spirits.

I recently attended a Comic-Con gathering with my teenage son Greyson. It is a place of wildly creative people. Many wear the costumes of their favorite super heroes. At one point, he turned to me and said, "Dad, these are my kind of people." What he sensed was the longing for a story that mattered. Where everyone had the ability to use his or her powers for good . . . if they chose to do so. A place where the stakes were high, because, to quote a famous web slinger, with great power comes great responsibility. Though we weren't in costume and didn't resonate with every story that played out, we sensed a common hunger. And we felt at home.

My daughter Hope loves basketball. Individually, she is an incredible player. Each girl on the team has her own unique talent and personality, but something exponentially more occurs when they step on the court together. They intuitively know where the other will throw the ball, or when to take the shot. They move as one without losing their individual essence. And what no person can do alone, five together can. On the court with these friends, she is at home.

That mirrors how Mia feels at this bohemian celebration. To be surrounded by people who live, love, and create from a place of freedom obtained from relationship with God, to have a place at the table, to savor the stories of others, and to celebrate your talents as a gift from the Creator. It is a feast for the soul.

That is the goal—and the promise—that awaits every son and daughter of God who enters the Freedom Realm.

It is a place where you can approach your life, your relationships, and your creativity with peace, joy, and passion.

You are expectant, regardless of what each day brings.

Your heart is fully awakened, alive and present to God and others.

You know who you are *and* who you are not. People or projects no longer have the power to validate, limit, or define you.

And you have discovered the only way to do life is with God and with others.

Living like this ushers in an atmosphere of abundance and freedom. There's no longer a need to try and control your Story. You know God has even bigger plans than you for what's ahead. So you are content to ride with Him wherever the path may lead.

Though much is accomplished here, it is less about what you do than who you are. It's a place where you never need to do more to feel less alone.

One word of caution. This life of freedom isn't about satisfying selfish desires. There are no

It's a place where you never need to do more to feel less alone. narcissists in the Freedom Realm. And it isn't about gritting your teeth, holding on, and making it through the day with a forced smile. That's simply faking it from your own strength. It's also not enough to have factual knowledge about the Freedom Realm. You get no points for talking a good game. No, you must step fully into it. And the only way to do that is to embrace life with the Creator.

This is the Freedom Realm. And it is available right where we are. As Iona said, "It is a state of the mind and a place of the heart."

with

"What's wrong, Mia?"

"I . . . don't know. I found myself in a place that I didn't want to be. I wanted to change it. But then, it changed me. And now that Story feels more real than my home here."

"Then re-create it here, Mia. By your choices each day. The goal was never to permanently escape this world. It was to discover how to live differently in it. Home is where you abide. When you do life with the Creator, you have found your true home."

"But I still don't know what happened to my dad. Spending time with him in Story was a gift, but—" Mia's eyes grew wide. *A gift.* Her hand went to her back pocket. The leather journal her dad had given her was still there. She set it on the table, incredulous that it made it back.

"You seem surprised."

"I'm confused. If the events of the Story weren't real, how did the journal make it back with me?"

"You knew the consequences within Story were real. Your transformation was real. Is it so hard to believe his gift could be real?"

Mia opened the cover to read her dad's handwritten note. "He told me this was for all the adventures we'd share together. Now all these pages will remain blank." As she flipped through the journal, a small piece of paper from inside fell to the table. It was the bookmark her dad had slid in the journal while they were in his truck.

Except it wasn't a bookmark. It was a name tag.

Mia froze. It was the same type name tag the old man in the forest had given her. She looked at Iona, unsure what to say.

"Perhaps your father left you a way to find him after all."

"That's impossible. I'd have recognized him. That man in the forest is too old to be my dad."

"His situation has aged him beyond his years. When he was in Story, Asher convinced him that your life was in peril, Mia. It was a lie. He knew if your father tried to pull out of the Story it would literally bring his world to a stop. In the desert, the construct imploded around him. Your father was thrown back in the forest, his mind fractured."

"But why would that affect his memory?"

"When you refuse to face your Story and your scars, you eventually forget who you are. For him, that loss could've happened almost immediately given the way he was ripped from Story. With no memory of where his truck was or who he was, he likely stayed put because it was the only place he felt safe."

"Or because O'Neal trapped him there. The raven brought him food but said bad things would happen if he left."

Iona poured a glass of water from the pitcher. "He didn't want your father to find help . . . or remember you."

Mia frowned. "If you knew he was here, why haven't you rescued him?"

"I help people see their Stories in new ways. I did that for your father. But I can't rescue people from their choices. That is the Creator's role. And He is now taking what the enemy tried to use against your father all those years ago — and using it to save him."

"What is that?"

"You."

"But you could have told me all this when we first met. He was just down the path."

"You weren't ready. Now that you have tasted true freedom, you can help others find their Story and freedom . . . and you get to start with your dad."

"By myself?"

"With the Creator. Hold on, I've got something for your trip." Iona headed to the barn on the other side of her yard. While she was gone, Mia retrieved her backpack and put the journal in it. Iona returned minutes later carrying a metal gas can.

"For your car."

Mia put her hands on her hips. "Why didn't you give me this earlier?"

"Because that wasn't what was needed." Iona walked Mia to her front porch. "Your adventure is just beginning, Mia."

"You know, I'm starting to believe that. Thank you, Iona."

The two embraced one last time. Then Mia headed down the path to her father. A backpack slung over her shoulder and a gas can in her hand.

Was it only yesterday that she was on this path about to meet Iona? As Mia got to the place where her father's truck was, she paused and thought of their drive to the diner. The journal he'd given her was in her backpack. Maybe it didn't have to stay empty after all. She put her hand on the hood. Then continued walking.

Mia spoke aloud to the Creator. "I'm not sure what to do. This whole journey, all I've wanted to do is find my father. And he's been here all the time."

As I have, Mia. Even when you lived as an Orphan, I was here for you. You've always been my daughter."

Mia nodded. "No matter what happens with my dad, I love having You as my Father."

Are you ready to see your dad?

"I'm afraid he won't ever remember me. Is he going to be okay?"

He's My son.

"I know, but he's been alone in the forest for almost twenty-five years."

His choices led to much loss, but he's never been alone.

Mia?

"Yes?"

We're here.

A few yards off the path, her father sat staring into the flickering campfire.

Mia set the gas can down and walked to the small fire. "Hi."

The old man looked at her through glassy eyes. "Are you lost?"

"Not anymore."

He stood slowly. "Who are you?"

"I'm Mia." She shook his frail hand.

"I'm not so good at names. Why are you crying?"

"Because . . . I've missed you so much."

The old man scratched his beard. "I think you've mistaken me for someone else." He shuffled to his bag. "Let me get you a name tag."

"I actually brought one for you." When he turned around, she was holding the name tag from her journal.

"Where'd you get that?"

"From my dad. We were really close."

"He sounds like a good man." The piece of paper shook in his hand. He looked at it and then at Mia. "I don't know my name."

"I do. May I?"

He handed her the pen. She uncapped it and wrote DAD.

He stared at the name a long time. Then put it on his shirt. "I was a dad once."

"What happened?"

"I can't remember."

"I think I can help you with that. I just found out who I am."

"Your name?"

"My identity. I'm a daughter of the Creator. And"—she paused and took a deep breath—"I'm also your daughter."

Tears fell from the old man's glassy eyes. "I wish I could remember that."

She began to cry as well. "It's been a long time since we got to live that way. But I've never stopped being your girl." Mia paused and took a deep breath. "I'm here to take you home, Dad."

"But this is—"

"No, I mean your real home."

"The raven won't like it. He says I have to stay here. If I don't –"

"Bad things happen, right? Well don't worry about him." Mia looked at the glow within the scar on her palm and thought back to when Ryder knocked O'Neal from the sky with a bolt of kintsugi. "He won't be an issue."

"But he did feed me."

"There's far better food."

Her dad gave her a puzzled look. "So what now?"

"We have a choice. We can return to my car with this gas can. It's just a few miles down the road. Or . . . I can show you something far more fantastical down a less traveled path."

He grinned. "I like the second choice."

Mia took his weathered hand in hers. "Come on Dad, let's find your Story. Together."

the shift
to with

HOME

It was telling when Mia told the Creator, "This whole journey, all I wanted to do is find my father. And he's been here all the time."

The reality is that even when we've felt like an orphan, we never were. Because though we lived as if we were alone, God was always there.

It's possible to be homesick for a home we never knew existed. At the deepest level, our desire for a home isn't actually for a physical dwelling place. But rather, a place where we are fully known. Not where we were born but where we can finally and fully be who we were created to be.

Our longing for home is actually our longing for God. That's why everyone who lives without God lives as an orphan. As Iona tells Mia, "When you do life with the Creator, you have found your true home." If He is our home, then as long as we

When you live *with* God, you are home regardless of your location.

try to do life on our own, we remain "homeless".

When you live *with* God, you are home regardless of your location. It is a place that doesn't require us to do more in order to belong. It is a place that we cannot lose or earn. Because everyone there is a much loved son or daughter of the Father.

Welcome home.

PART THREE

end
of the
beginning

Changes Along the Way

We entered into this Story . . . for your Story. And your freedom.

Iona gave Mia the chance to step into a most fantastical journey. It didn't simply get her from Point A to Point B. It offered her a new realm to live from.

I extend the same invitation to you. Go on a search for your Story...and your Father. It's the rare trip where you'll return with less baggage than when you started. Because life in the Freedom Realm is so much simpler, enjoyable, and exciting than what those in the Orphan Realm face. And a huge reason

> When you no longer try to control the navigation, you can actually breathe easier and enjoy the journey.

why is because when you no longer try to control the navigation, you can actually breathe easier and enjoy the journey.

The four vials revealed a better way for Mia, and for us, to approach life.

The first contained ocean water and showed her how to stay expectant for future waves.

The second held the scent of Mia's dream and reminded her to pursue it from an awakened heart.

The third surged with the healing glow of kintsugi to help Mia discover her identity and the strength of her scars once they are redeemed.

And the fourth contained the words of her dad's love so she'll never forget to take this journey together with her Father.

When fused together, these vials echo the invitation from Psalm 27:14.

"Stay with God.
Take Heart; Don't Quit.
I'll say it again, Stay with God!"
(The Message)

This is what it comes down to—staying with God, awakening our hearts, and not giving up. Notice that one command is repeated. Stay with God. I think the psalmist starts and ends with these three words because nothing is more essential. This the foundation of our journey. "With." That is what it all comes down to. We will either do life with or without God. Nothing is more essential, and, unfortunately, nothing is easier for us to forget when the next shiny opportunity appears. So the psalmist reminds us . . . stay with God.

Be Expectant

The first vial was named *Expectant* for a reason.

Let that be how you live each day from this moment forward. The unplanned interruptions. The unfulfilled desire. The fractured relationship with a loved one. Awake each morning and lay your head on the pillow each evening with a sense of, "Where are you in this, Father?" Before I get out of bed each morning and get lost in the day, I first find myself in God. It's amazing how tensions and worry decrease when I focus on God rather than the problem. I'm not demanding answers or a specific outcome. It's the ability to take things in without being taken out by them. The key is to simply remain expectant for what He is up to as you approach the demands of the day together.

If God has given you a dream, He will see it through. He doesn't stir a desire in us to leave it unfulfilled. Now, the way He brings it to being may be totally different than you imagined, or even wanted it to be. That's

> If God has given you a dream, He will see it through.

why it's essential to keep your heart expectant rather than set on rigid expectations. There's a world of difference in those two postures.

You must release the illusion of control as you step into mystery and strange new lands with God. This guarantees the unexpected. Once you believe anything can happen, you're open to whatever God invites you into. Often these will be situations you couldn't have imagined with outcomes only possible through Him.

Carry an Adventure Journal

Mia's dad gave her a leather journal. It stirred a sense of expectancy for what was to come and all they would experience together.

You need a similar notebook of expectancy for your adventures with God.

My suggestion is to buy a journal exclusively for this purpose. While there are digital options available, I encourage you to invest in a physical, tangible journal. There's something organic and real about pen on paper in your handwriting. When you run out of pages, it's time to start the next. Keep the completed journals on a shelf reserved for your most prized possessions. When you begin to doubt God's goodness or faithfulness, pull out one of your earlier journals...and remember.

> You need a similar notebook of expectancy for your adventures with God.

When I speak at events, I sometimes give attendees a spiral notebook. It's the kind students buy for a few bucks. What makes it priceless is what happens next. Before the gathering, I turn to the first page and ask God what He'd like to say to the person who will receive this journal. Sometimes it's a word. Other times, a few sentences or a verse from the Bible. It's the equivalent of an inscription, like the one Mia's dad wrote to her. Except this is from your Father…to you.

The entire process requires a huge amount of trust and faith. The spiritual equivalent of walking on a tightrope over the Grand Canyon blindfolded. It is all up to God, but I have to step out in faith and count on Him to get me to the other side.

The reason I do this is because it breaks through the fog that many have when it comes to hearing from God. It's impossible to do life with God if you don't believe He has anything to say to you. What good father would never speak directly or intimately to his children, but expect them to go through all of life reading his letters and figuring out how that advice or command applies to their every decision?

Yet many go through their entire life believing we only hear from God through Scripture. The problem

with that is the very Scripture they look to is over-
flowing with stories of God speaking to the hearts
of His followers. And He hasn't lost His voice.
God's children are invited to listen to His voice
(John 10:3-4). He primarily speaks in a way that we
can hear internally. His words will never contradict
Scripture, but they will be personal and specific
to your situation. If you struggle with this issue, let
me pose a simple question. You may not think God
does speak, but would you want to hear His voice if
He did? Is the desire there? If so, that is enough. Ask
Him and be both expectant and patient. I think you
may just be amazed at what happens from there.

Others long to hear from God, but then discredit
the words because they sound too good to be
true. They assume it must be their own self-talk.

But this exercise breaks through that barrier.
Because what each person receives isn't something they came up with. I often don't know what
a particular message means from God when I
write the words. When it's time to hand the notebooks out, I don't know who will receive which
journal. I actively wait for His guidance. I sense
the woman to my right should get the first book in

my hands. The gentleman next to her, the green one two-thirds down in the stack. And on it goes until every person has a notebook.

As I watch people open their notebooks and read the words the Father longs for them to hear, the moment is almost too holy to describe. It is if an ocean of grace washes through the room as His words wash over them. Because the very words they thought were too good to be true are right there.

I invite you to go through a similar process with your adventure journal. Get away from the noise of the world and ask God what He'd like to inscribe in your journal. Remember, these aren't words you are coming up with. They are His. And His words are always unique and personal. If what comes to you sounds like a generic greeting card, that's probably not God's voice. He is intimate. He is also disruptive. His words may surprise you but they will never bore you. They will never condemn you. They will stir your soul.

If you initially don't hear His voice within your spirit, stay with it. There's no pressure for this to happen immediately. Come back to it the next day. The enemy hates this process, so if you hear words that you know are lies, it's important to remember God isn't the only one who speaks. Resist the enemy and command him— and the fog he often ushers in— to leave. And keep in mind that we can often hear better for oth-

His words may surprise you but they will never bore you. They will never condemn you. They will stir your soul.

ers than we can for ourselves, especially when it involves high-stakes decisions or long-term desires.

As powerful as the upfront words from God are, the pages that follow are even more so. The blank pages signify the stories that have yet to be written. They are the adventures the two of you have yet to live.

I invite you to spend some time with God on the following questions.

1. God, what do You think of me?

2. You've given me a specific talent and passion, so why does it often feel like this dream will never become a reality?

3. What dreams for my future do I approach as though it is 100 percent up to me? How can I move from independence to full dependence on You for these desires?

4. Does my validation really come from You, God, or from how others respond (or don't) to what I offer?

5. God, expose areas of my life where I still cling to control. Help me learn the art of letting go what I don't control anyway.

6. This journey isn't just about discovering your true identity. Ask God about His identity. You are who you are because God is first who He is. Get to know Him. Not as an academic study but as you would a best friend. Spend time in Scripture. Spend time with Him. Ask questions. Look at how His many names (Creator, Provider, I Am) reveal specific traits about His character. He is the most fascinating being ever. And you get to spend your life together.

Don't rush through these questions. And remember, even though you are creative, the goal isn't for you to create your own answers. It is just the opposite. Only write what God stirs in your soul. His answer may be a word, a sentence, or pages of insight. It may be playful, poetic or serious. Don't try to filter or rewrite His words. Whatever He says, capture it in the journal even if it doesn't make immediate sense.

Those brave enough to carry a travel journal for their adventures with God reveal hearts of expectancy. There is such freedom when you live in this posture of expectancy while letting go of all your expectations. There's no demand on how the Story of your life will go. Relinquish the script you've been holding so tight and replace it with an expectancy for all God desires. Not just for you but that He wants to do with you.

> Those brave enough to carry a travel journal for their adventures with God reveal hearts of expectancy.

The journal reminds you of the adventure you are on with God. There will be pages of all the two of you did together, of all the rescues, of all the ways your Father delighted you, of questions yet to be answered, of times of wrestling and times of wonder. In that way, the journal will also strengthen you when the enemy tries to convince you that you're all alone. You will immediately know it's a lie because before you is the Story of your journey with God. And when you're with Him, you are never alone.

Awaken Your Heart

The second vial is *Awaken* because only when your heart is awakened will you know what to pursue. Before that, you will be searching for ways to fill your broken heart rather than offer from a heart that is fully alive.

Only when your heart is awakened will you know what to pursue.

Mia loves to cook. This stirred her heart from the time she was a young girl. Yet that desire was constantly opposed. She dreamed of being a chef, but the world told her to get busy doing a job. Just follow the rules and be productive.

We've all faced situations where we feel simultaneously overwhelmed with life and yet underwhelmed at what it has to offer. What we most desire doesn't happen. Or it does but the emptiness remains. Worse, we give our heart to someone or some cause and it gets trampled.

Mia had shut her heart down. But then she got a taste of what could be when she stepped into the bohemian kitchen. She was suddenly in the presence of like-minded people. Then she experienced even greater fellowship at the rooftop gathering. What had seemed impossible before was now a reality.

> We've all faced situations where we feel simultaneously overwhelmed with life and yet underwhelmed at what it has to offer.

The same can happen for you.

Perhaps you've let go of what used to bring you such joy. Or you find yourself going through each day in a job that pays the bills, but doesn't stimulate your heart. Some say it's impossible or extremely rare to find a job that can do both. Perhaps. But why not be one of the rare ones?

If you haven't found your calling yet, don't believe for a minute that you don't have one. If that is you, my suggestion is to find God before you try to find your talent. Spend time with Him. And see what the two of you will discover together on the playground of possibilities. He may surprise you by inviting you into something you never imagined doing and yet now can't imagine doing anything else.

Here's another way to shed light on your truer calling. When you think back on your Story, what have you always been drawn to? I'm not asking what others say you're good at. We can be good at doing things that we have little interest in. I'm talking about activities that cause you to lose track of time when you enter into them. What would it look like to experience that joy again, in a fresh new way? Perhaps you are closer to discovering your truer calling than you think.

> Perhaps you are closer to discovering your truer calling than you think.

I know an eye surgeon. He restores sight. That's his profession and he's good at it. But one day he realized if money wasn't an issue, he'd write stories. That felt like such a disconnect from the trajectory of his career. I pointed out that there was actually a clear link between the two. His passion was to help people see. That was his true calling. But his deeper love was writing stories. Rather than a detour from what he'd been doing, God was inviting him to help people see in an entirely new way—through story. That is his truer calling.

Or consider the fishermen before they met Jesus in Galilee. They excelled at their craft. Fishing likely brought these men some level of joy, but then Jesus invited them into something truer. In an instant, expert fishermen became "fishers of men." They traded the foreshadowing of their prior calling for a full measure of what they were born to be. Their truer calling.

The enemy does not want us to awaken to our truer calling with God. He's happy to play any song we want other than the theme song of our life . . . the one that God sings over us. The enemy hates when you discover that song instead of the playlist that lulls your soul into mere duty and obligation.

But it all begins with your heart. That's why, as noted earlier, Scripture tells us we need to protect, guard, and nurture our heart above all else. You will never experience the fantastical or be able to care for the hearts of others if your own heart is numb. But once it awakens to the beauty of life with God, look out!

Know Your Identity

This is who you are. And how can you be true to God, others, or even yourself before you've settled this? The only way out of the desert is to know your identity. That is why *Identity* is the third vial.

> Identity never hinges in what you do. It is unconditionally based on who you are.

Identity never hinges in what you do. It is unconditionally based on who you are. If the foundation of your identity isn't secure as a son or daughter of God, it is likely an identity tied to an addiction or wound.

There are at least four significant forces that can diminish your God-given identity:

1. The world tries to define you. At any gathering, the most common question is, "What do you do?"

   Over time, we learn to do more of what gets noticed or rewarded and avoid what we don't do well. The world focuses on productivity rather than presence. The external rather than the internal. Doing over being. Your business title hinges on what you do. Your income may as well. Many relationships, including marriage, are, unfortunately, based on performance.

2. The enemy tries to destroy us (John 10:10). As discussed earlier, he chose the wrong story and does everything in his power to cause us to do the same.

3. Our fears limit us. We legitimize and rationalize our phobias and worries rather than believe that it's possible to live without them. They aren't just a bad habit, they keep us from living in freedom.

4. Isolation neuters us. That's why those in the Orphan Realm often forget who they are. You simply cannot fully enter into identity if you do life alone.

All of these can erode our identity, yet none of them have the authority to name us.

Only the Creator can name His creation. And God has named us. He is our Father and we are His sons and daughters (2 Corinthians 6:18). And unlike a name or title the world gives, this identity can never be lost, stolen, or downgraded.

As His son or daughter, you have total access to an all-knowing, all-powerful, all-loving, really good dad.

"Chase" Success

I wish you success on your journey but your validation is not tied to success. The truth is, no one can guarantee that any of your ventures will ever attain worldly success. Even when everything aligns, the result is short-term happiness at best.

The enemy loves to keep changing the definition of success so it never quite arrives. Every time you achieve one victory, it vanishes and the next challenge is set before you. The pursuit of this is life on a treadmill that speeds up but doesn't ever take you anywhere but to a state of exhaustion.

Success also isn't determined by other's responses or even your own expectations. Say you were to create or design or write something with God that is beyond your wildest dreams—and then He whispers to you, "That was just for the two of us. It's not something to share with the world." If it stopped there, would it be enough? After all, it's something you created with the Creator of the universe. It was born from shared intimacy. That's huge. But is it enough?

> Success also isn't determined by other's responses or even your own expectations.

Rather than giving us a formula for success, God instead gives us Himself. Formulas don't require God's presence. Worse, they offer the illusion of control in place of intimacy and dependence on a wild, unpredictable, playful, non-formulaic Creator.

So while discipline, craft, productivity, and hard work are helpful tools, they can only take you so far. So yes, master your craft and grow in your specific industry. But also make sure your day is driven more by His eternal rhythms than any external results that can be achieved without God.

This surpasses every technique known to humans. While people can teach the mechanical, you are invited to experience the mysterious. That is what bohemians in the Freedom Realm discover.

I mentioned at the start of this book that there was only one definition of success that could be guaranteed. Here it is:

Stay *with* God and experience all that happens today as his son or daughter.

That's it. The man or woman who does that is successful. And at peace.

My youngest son Chase showed me this simple truth. I have a big truck. Every time I get in it, he is ready to join me. He articulated the theme of this entire book in a single sentence during a recent trip: "I don't care what we do as long as we do it together." That's the posture we need to take with God. Wherever He's going, we're in.

And you know what? For every trip, my son's success ratio is 100 percent. Because no matter where we go, he achieves his desire. To be with his father.

Notice something else about this posture. He doesn't link success to what happens on the trip. There is such freedom in this. You'll never again need to wait until an adventure is over to determine if it was a success. But if he tied success to whether we got home without a flat tire, or if he got an ice cream cone, or if I paid him to help me with a chore, well then, the reward lies in something other than being together. But if the only goal is being together, then that reward is guaranteed every time. I could surprise him and take him to his favorite store. Or a movie. And I often do. But even then, the bonus never is more important than the intimacy of being together.

Don't let the hope of some other reward distract you from the real prize. Rest in that definition of success and you'll experience it every time. Guaranteed.

Do It Together

The antidote to being an orphan and doing life "without God" is simple. It is to do life—all of life—"with God". I'm convinced nothing is more important.

That is why the final vial is *Together*.

In Mia's story, this vial held her dad's words. It is the sound of intimacy. The voice of our Father. And ultimately, the only way she could enter the Freedom Realm was by stepping through the Blue Door together, with God.

Staying with God infers intimacy but also dependence. We are not meant to do it on our own. We need God and others along the way. The rooftop gathering in Mia's journey brings to life the sort of creative fellowship that I've long dreamed of being a part of. It's a mythic version of a specific desire.

Rather than only surrounding myself with those who have the same talents, I want to have conversations with chefs, musicians, entertainers, and creative bohemians who pursue God and others through their calling. I envision a time in the future when I host "rooftop"events with a small group of people hungry to celebrate the Creator through their creativity and their Stories. A time to consecrate our creativity. A spiritual and literal feast for those who are committed to pursuing life, love, and creativity with God. A celebration of the rare ones. Perhaps I will see you there.

I'm expectant as to how God will breathe life into that dream.

But You Can't Do It All

You can do a lot. But you can't do it all.

But the world dangles endless choices before us. We're encouraged to do more, say more, try more, and achieve more.

The posters at the gym where I work out proclaim: "You Can Do It All." It plays to the illusion that we really can do it all and have it all *if* we just somehow learn to balance everything in our lives perfectly (or maybe join the right health club).

"You Can Do It All."

Except . . . you can't. It's not only impossible. It's cruel to even hold that out as the ideal.

You can put your family life above work. Or you can give your job top priority. You can overcommit and give many things a small piece of yourself. Or you can choose a life of simplicity. You can master a skill through patient dedication. Or you can let social media consume your day. But you can't balance the above items, much less everything else in your life.

> When you get down to it, only two things really matter. Love God. Love others.

And why is balance the goal anyway?

When you get down to it, only two things really matter. Love God. Love others. That means doing life a certain way. With God. With others. Give your best to your best. And just enough time to the other things that must be done.

Orphans go through most of their lives without God and without others. That's why they feel alone. But as Mia found out, both parts of the equation matter. A life with God but not others is dysfunctional. And a life focused on others yet lacking God's presence is missing the most important piece of all.

It often feels like there's not enough time in our day—or left in our life—to do what needs to be done. First, recognize that the prior sentence is a "doing" statement. And yes, while things need to get done, remember *being* always comes before *doing*. And this sense of "not enough time"? Do you really think the Creator of time won't give you time for what He's stirred you to do? Sure, it may look different than you imagined it would. But you can't be running behind when you are running with God. When you find the Creator of time, you find time. With God,

> Do you really think the Creator of time won't give you time for what He's stirred you to do?

you really do have all the time in the world.

You *do* have enough time for everything God calls you to. The bohemian fellowship calls that living a wildly unbalanced life. A balanced life is just another way of trying to control everything. Let that go and live completely unbalanced for the things that matter most.

That is the way to true intimacy. And the way to finally discover your true home. With God.

The Story of With

Before a new journey can truly begin anew, there must be an end to the status quo.

> Faith isn't needed at the victory party after the battle has been fought. It's needed in the middle of the "not yet."

If the best we can do during the challenging times is hunker down and hope for something better and easier, we miss living fully in every season of life. The time to trust and risk is now. Faith isn't needed at the victory party after the battle has been fought. It's needed in the middle of the "not yet." Can you be steadfast in the unknown, before you can see the horizon or know the test results or understand how the pieces fit together?

The focus of your journey changes when it becomes about relationships rather than either your inadequacies or your rewards.

Here's what it all comes down to. What kind of life do you want—a safe, predictable one or a story filled with mystery that forces you to lean into God? Which do you think will transform you into a person of depth and wisdom? Which life will people remember and talk about around campfires a hundred years from now?

This is an invitation to spend your lives pursuing what you most enjoy doing—together with God. Raising a family. Investing in your passion. Chasing your dreams. In all of it, God's primary goal isn't to teach you lessons. He's a Father who teaches, not a Teacher who fathers. And a Father's deepest desire is to invite his sons and daughters into more

He's a Father who teaches, not a Teacher who fathers.

> God didn't primarily create us so we would do things *for* Him. Or even to learn lessons *about* Him. His primary reason for creating us is so we can be *with* Him.

intimate relationship with Him. Which means God didn't primarily create us so we would do things *for* Him. Or even to learn lessons *about* Him. His primary reason for creating us is so we can be *with* Him.

So be that. Be a teacher. Be a poet. Be a basketball player. Be a ballerina. Be a spouse. Be a parent. Be whatever He is inviting you into—just do it *with* Him.

The life you have with God while creating determines the life your art or service will have. As your life grows closer to God through shared adventures, you are refined through testing, faith, and sacrifice. Which refines your talent and gifting.

In that way, our creativity reveals more about us than we think. What we give birth to—from ideas and stories to songs and medical breakthroughs—possesses both the strengths and the blind spots of the creator. You simply can't create some item or piece of art more powerful than your own life. Where you are faking it, your art will be less true. Where you haven't gone, your creations can't go.

This shift to *with* is essential. Miss that and you miss everything. Do it on your own and you do it all alone.

In Mia's story, she was given four vials. May you carry the same four reminders as you journey through your Story.

Stay Expectant.
Awaken Your Heart.
Know Your Identity.
Do It Together.

May they help you transition from the Orphan Realm to the Freedom Realm.

It's time to start that journey of freedom. Not tomorrow. Not next week. Right now.

You don't need more answers before you begin. You just need to be ready to ride.

Your Father drives a really big truck and the passenger seat is open. There's plenty of time to get to know each other. And to hear more of His story.

Don't forget to grab your journal on your way out. I have a feeling it's going to be a really good story.

acknowledgments

I am on a journey of sonship. And that has changed literally everything in my life for the better. I am discovering what love is. And from that, how to love God and love others. Thankfully, God has surrounded me with a wild fellowship of others who desire the same. My heart is full because of the names here.

God – I love being your son. Waking up each day expectant for your presence is my greatest joy. Any power this message has is from you. Any shortcomings are from me. To do this together with you was amazing.

To my wife Kellye – you take my breath away. In who you are, in how you love, and in your immense beauty. Love never ends.

To our children. Greyson – your passion for story made this a better story. The elevator and the raven scenes are what they are because of your encouragement and imagination. Hope – your voice and beauty astonish me. Even more, your heart for those the world overlooks reveals so much of God's desire for the orphans. Chase – your unquenchable joy in spending time together, no matter what we do, brings me immense joy as a Father, and shows me how to approach God as His son.

Craig McConnell – you initiated me into the concept of intimacy with God. And now you are face-to-face with Him. I will see you again my friend. Until then, I miss your presence.

To the Fellowship of Creative Bohemians. Without your continual belief, support, harassment, songs, and humor, this journey would have been far less fun and far more lonely. James L. Rubart – a decade ago, I didn't know what it could be like to have a friend closer than a brother. Now I do. Mary Weber – your invitation to lean into others revealed what Creative Fellowship could be. Your stories are amazing. Your friendship more so. In a word . . . Inagodadavida. Kristy Cambron – you experience God in ways that stir me into deeper intimacy with him. From verse-mapping to the deeper meaning of names and colors, you continue to taste and see that God is good. Jason Clark – a supposedly random scan of a bookshelf one afternoon led me to your first book (now titled *Untamed*). Though we've yet to meet in person, your songs, stories of sonship, and love of strong coffee have created a deep bond. Ted Dekker – we met through story. Dozens of books later, we have become friends within a greater story – the story of Yeshua. Katie Ganshert – you have such a passion for life, for joy, and for the unseen and forgotten. I so appreciate who you are. James Arnold Taylor – you are a man of a thousand voices, yet I savor your unique voice the most. Few can bring life to characters in a "galaxy far, far away" and to those right before them like you can. Betsy St. Amant – your life is a testimony to a daughter who hungers and thirsts for her Father no matter the circumstances. Stay in those deep waters and keep inviting others to join you there.

I also want to express deep appreciation to:

Clayton, Gale, Johnny, and Amy – it is a privilege to be your son and brother. Home is where all of our journeys begin. I have experienced your love and belief since day one. And still do.

And to friends who God used at just the right moments to keep this project alive. Rick Hinnant – thank you for opening your home to me that cold

November weekend. It was sacred ground where the final first draft of this book came into being. Ashley Clark, Susan Crawford, Doug DeChant, Gabe Jenkins, Becky Waggoner, and Brian Cohen – your friendship and belief in this project energized me. Bart Hanson – your encouragement and support helped bring this story to life when I was running on empty. You are such a good father to so many men. The entire Ransomed Heart team – we have been through so much together. I am in awe of your trueness and your great hearts as we pursue more of God. It's an honor to walk alongside you in this journey.

Natalie Hanemann, Kristen Ingebretson, and Lorie DeWorken – you each independently lent your creative gifting to help this story become a book. The talents and passion God has given each of you breathed life into the words, pages, and cover in ways that continue to astonish me. I am grateful. Rielynn Grace – your eye for photography is amazing. You didn't have much to work with but we had a blast taking head shots for the book.

May the best parts of our Stories be the chapters yet to be told!

There Is More

Pursuing life and creativity with God is beautifully disruptive and immensely freeing. It begins with knowing God as both Creator and Father...and ourselves as his sons and daughters.

If you're tired of trying to get things done in your own strength or make success happen by following yet another formula, that's good. Because there is a better way. One that will awaken your heart...and your art.

As a fellow traveler,
I hope you'll join me in that journey.

To discover more, visit **withallen.com**

ALLEN ARNOLD
Author of *The Story of With* and *Waves of Creativity*

CHAOS CAN'T

Overcome What Comes Against You in This Shaken World

Stepping into the Unknown

This book began with my journey for answers. In many ways, it follows the trajectory of the traditional hero's journey.

Let me be quick to say I'm not the hero of this journey. Whether we realize it or not, God is the deepest longing of all our searches, the hero of every quest for more life.

The unexpected turns that we'll encounter aren't a surprise to God. He regularly invites us into the new and unknown. What we can miss is how his invitations are often initiations. God prepares us for coming opportunities by showing us how to master things beyond our current abilities. We'll never be ready for what's next as long as we're determined to hold tightly to the now.

Richard Niebuhr said, "Pilgrims are poets who create by taking journeys." Initiation is in the DNA of every hero's journey. If you're not familiar with the term, it was coined by literature professor Joseph Campbell in 1949. It refers to a mythic cycle that the protagonist of practically every story follows, whether *Star Wars*, *The Matrix*, *Beauty and the Beast*, or *Lord of the Rings*.

There are countless variations, but at a base level, every hero's journey involves an ordinary person choosing to step from the known to the unknown. Doing so requires the help of a sage, an onslaught of challenges, confrontation with the abyss where all seems lost (at the midpoint of the journey), discovering gifts and powers, and ultimately overcoming through some form of death and rebirth. The hero's journey rings true for characters in a story because these same stages are true for the stories we are living. These journeys create a change in us. We begin seeing life one way, but by the last mile, we're no longer the same. We don't just arrive somewhere new. We arrive a different person, transformed by the journey.

It always begins with a tug toward the unknown. It did for me. I was just trying to get through my days. But as the chaos increased, I could feel the negative impact on my heart and my art, on who I am and what I do. I knew chaos was trying to keep me imprisoned, numb to my true calling.

I'm reminded of this quote from the thirteenth-century Persian poet Hafiz: "The small man builds cages for everyone he knows—while the Sage, who has to duck his head when the moon is low, keeps dropping keys all night long for the beautiful, rowdy prisoners."

Chaos rages as God relentlessly drops keys for those the enemy tries to keep captive. Once we are awakened and set free, we can't help but join God in offering light and life to others.

Eventually, I had enough. God dropped me a key and invited me into more. So I set out—with him—for answers.

I'll admit, part of my motive was a deep desire to defeat chaos. Not singlehandedly, like King Arthur slaying the dragon. Though that would be cool. Rather, I wanted to defeat it in my realm. For me and those I love. I wanted my heart—and my creativity—back.

That was more than enough motivation to get me started.

I quickly found myself in way over my head. But that's okay. Unless you choose to stay forever in a small story, you have to undertake adventures where you're no longer the expert. That's why these journeys require a sage.

On this quest, God is our sage. Why do we need his wisdom on this topic when there are countless teachings on how to bring more calm to our lives? Because no one has ever responded better to chaos than God, Jesus, and the Spirit. Nor does any human have the eternal understanding of what's really going on.

"The small man builds cages for
everyone he knows—while the
Sage, who has to duck his head
when the moon is low, keeps
dropping keys all night long for
the beautiful, rowdy prisoners."

—*Hafiz*

What We're After

My hope is that this quest will reveal:

- why chaos hits in such personal ways;
- how to not let the swirling outside chaos . . . within;
- the possible origin of chaos;
- how to counter fear with love;
- why your creativity matters more than you imagine; and
- 11 ways to restore your dreams and renew your surroundings.

I enter into this as an explorer, not as an expert. I'm not always sure where the next turn is but am confident the journey is a worthy one. As Henry Nouwen says, "Answers before questions do harm to the soul." Theologians smarter than I have spent thousands of years debating many of the things we'll consider. Yet none can be definitive, because none were there at creation. They're trying to make sense of things. As are we.

I'm inviting you to follow me in this journey of discovery. Along the way, I'll do my best to ask good questions and then follow them as far as I can. I'm not a theologian. I'm simply a man who has discovered and accepted God's wild invitation to do life actively with him. That's how I'm approaching this. As a shared adventure. One with huge implications for how we interpret our lives and hold on to our dreams.

My hope is you'll also embrace a sense of expectancy, curiosity, and childlike wonder. If you disagree with a point or two, that's okay. No human has all the answers. Not everything can be diagrammed into a nice chart. No matter how we wish otherwise, eternal questions and the mysteries of God simply don't work that way. God loves it when we seek after him and his ways.

> But without faith it is impossible to please Him, for he who comes to God must believe that He is, and that He is a rewarder of those who diligently seek Him. (Hebrews 11:6 NKJV)

Diligently seeking is what we're doing here. My hunch is if we trust God to guide us, we can better understand the cause of chaos and move to the cure.

Before we get started, I want to offer you some hope:

- The Creator is never surprised or worried about chaos.
- God created you for such a time as this. You can overcome chaos.
- Neither the storms nor the scars get the final word. God does.

Yes, in this moment, chaos can do some real damage. But it can't overpower God. There is a way to overcome what comes against you.

It is possible to live chaos-free in a world filled with chaos. That's what we're after.

How Are You Doing?

Imagine you're sitting around a campfire deep in the middle of a calm forest. You're in a small circle of fellow travelers. The faces are peaceful yet there's a shared intensity. Everyone here has lost something to chaos. And has a desire to overcome it.

The logs in the fire pop and crackle. It's not a time for small talk. It's a moment to look up at the shimmering stars—as well as deep into your heart.

Why did you pick up this book? What is it you hope for this journey?

Chaos comes in a variety of sizes and flavors. It hits in ways we never saw coming. It affects our health, finances, marriage, friendships, faith, family, and dreams. The trail of devastation can result in the loss of a job, the loss of hope, the loss of patience, or even the loss of life.

After numerous encounters, we develop a low-level dread of the next news alert, the bill in the mail, or even what tomorrow holds. Just getting through the day becomes our goal.

So let's name the things you're struggling with in this season. What chaos is swirling in your world? What is being lost or stolen because of it? Write your answers in the space on the next page. Naming something is a way to show it matters, and this matters immensely.

Take a moment to name the things you're struggling with in this season. What chaos is swirling in your world? What is being lost or stolen because of it?

_____

_____

_____

_____

_____

_____

_____

_____

_____

_____

_____

_____

There's no prize for the least or most chaotic experiences. Nor does experience make experts in how to overcome it. So don't get sidetracked. The goal is to gain true freedom from chaos while having compassion *for*—but not comparison *to*—others who are struggling.

Chaos looks and impacts each of us differently. Some is global. There are natural disasters, wars and rumors of wars, viruses, violence, social unrest, self-serving politicians, false prophets, and economic collapse. Some hits far closer to home in the form of cancer or depression. Facing life without a loved one. Financial struggles. A toxic relationship with a boss, spouse, child, or parent. Maybe your chaos is the nonstop to-do list that leaves no time for rest or soul care.

You may be facing chaos on several fronts at once. If you're in a rare reprieve, I'm happy for you. But I'm also here to tell you it won't last. We don't live in paradise.

Chaos hits each of us differently. Yet curiously, it seeks the same thing from each of us. Let's see why.

Unless you choose to stay forever
in a small story, you have to
undertake adventures where
you're no longer the expert.

The Toll It Takes

It's helpful to note how chaos usually begins.
Almost always, it starts with an external event that tries to move internally.

You get a panicked call from your friend. A diagnosis from your doctor. A past-due bill you thought you'd paid. An inflammatory comment on social media.

That external situation snags you in its vortex as it accelerates. Then that chaotic swirling tries to get inside your head and your heart.

To cope, we find ways to ignore, numb, or medicate the craziness. We're desperate for relief.

Yet it never seems to come. Not really. The toll chaos takes on our lives is catastrophic. It tries to infuse us with fear, shut down our heart, steal our hope, destroy our dreams, and erode our creativity. It affects us physically, mentally, emotionally, relationally, and spiritually.

I'm sorry for what it has cost you. Though I've never walked in your shoes, I hope this message can offer hope in the midst of your storms.

I was being taken out on multiple fronts. As a writer, I showed up at my keyboard. But the words didn't come. A void was overtaking my imagination. It was like my creativity was freefalling into a huge hole.

I'm not alone on that front. I coach a lot of creative individuals and groups. They have experienced the same thing. Even though they have deep passions, in times of chaos they lose interest in their pursuits. Their focus wanes.

I tried everything to escape chaos. I ignored it, hoping it would go away. If only. I attempted to control it, which just made my world grow smaller. I pretended it didn't affect me, which wasn't true—and later caused me to feel both hopeless and foolish. I hunkered down to wait it out, but passivity can't overcome the storms of life.

What do you do when everything hits the fan? Who do you become? I'm guessing you've tried various ways to manage or deal with the havoc.

Let's expose unhelpful behaviors by naming them.

CPSIA information can be obtained
at www.ICGtesting.com
Printed in the USA
LVHW012055280622
722308LV00007B/225